Progressive Basketball Drills: A Coach's Guide

Don Edmonston

Jack Lehane

WITHDRAWN

Allyn and Bacon, Inc.

Boston • London • Sydney • Toronto

The authors dedicate the book to one another. Only because of their friendship, their similar philosophies, and styles of coaching could this work have been accomplished.

Secondly, Coach Edmonston dedicates the book to his wife Marcia and their four children. Coach Lehane dedicates the book to his parents for their support and to Gabriele.

Finally, a special dedication to Coach Edmonston's wife Marcia. Much gratitude and appreciation for her help and support in the preparation of this manuscript.

Library of Congress Cataloging in Publication Data

Edmonston, Don.
  Progressive basketball drills.

  1. Basketball—Training. 2. Basketball—Coaching.
I. Lehane, Jack, 1935–   . II. Title.
GV885.35.E35 1984 796.32'3'077 83–19666
ISBN 0–205–08064–2

Printed in the United States of America

10 9 8 7 6 5 4 3 2 1 87 86 85 84 83

Contents

Foreword

Most professional people have several sourcebooks in their possession for easy reference, but what does the basketball coach have available on the topic of basketball drills? Edmonston and Lehane have pulled together "more than you ever wanted to know" about basketball drills under one cover for the convenience of the teacher of basketball.

The uniqueness of this book is not the originality of the drills, but rather the cumulation of materials for reference. Thought has been given to logical progression of drills, and basketball coaches at all levels will be able to get many good ideas from the text.

Tom Davis
Stanford University

Preface

The basic premise of this book is that in basketball the better individual players and the more successful teams are fundamentally better prepared. Our opinion is that inaividual and team skills should be developed to the highest level and that the best method of teaching fundamentals is through drills. The main objective of the book is to provide coaches with a concise and comprehensive handbook of drills that have proven to be successful teaching aids. The drills that we present contain some that have been used universally for years, some that are variations of the basics, and some that have been recently introduced. We emphasize that there are no secrets in basketball coaching and that it is difficult to know the origin of all drills used by the thousands of coaches who work at the game. There is an endless number of drills available, as each coach devises drills that meet his or her team's needs.

Some drills are concerned with helping to teach one particular aspect of a fundamental, and many include several fundamentals. After teaching individual fundamentals in separate drills, a coach may use drills that combine these fundamentals. The drills should be progressive in degree of difficulty as the skills of the players progress. Also, the time of year (early, middle, or late season) is often a determining factor in selecting the difficulty of a drill as well as in deciding how the drills may be combined so that less time is used in a practice session. Because we believe that drills should be varied daily, or as often as possible to avoid monotony, we have tried to present a number of drills that will teach the same fundamental(s).

Drills by themselves will not answer all questions or solve all coaching problems. Coaches must know the purpose of a drill, make corrections when necessary, and have the patience to repeat the drill as often as necessary until the particular skill has been learned.

Team and Individual Conditioning

INTRODUCTION

The purpose of this chapter is to present to the coach a variety of drills that will provide methods to improve players' stamina (endurance), alertness, reactions, quickness, speed and strength. As the coach prepares a team for the upcoming season, he may realize that the team has offensive and/or defensive deficiencies, but conditioning, or lack of it, should not be the difference between winning and losing.

The drills are recommended for use when a coach has the teams together after the squads have been selected and the size of the team determined.

Each coach will use these drills and others of his own choosing or design to prepare his team both physically and mentally for the strenuous and demanding basketball season. All drills may be used regardless of the philosophy of the coaching staff. For example, fast-break teams as well as slow-break (possession-type) teams will benefit from their use. These drills may also be combined with other aspects of team basketball so as to allow coaches and teams who have time and space restrictions to accomplish more within these limitations. The majority of the conditioning drills will be explained, and a few of the drills will be diagramed.

TEAM LAPS AND SPRINTS

Drill 1   Indian File Running

1. Players are placed in a single file along the outside of the baseline.
2. Player 1 leads the line and runs at a pace determined by the coach. All other players follow as they move around the court on the outside of the baselines and sidelines.
3. On the coach's signal (whistle or voice) player 10 sprints from his position to take the lead. The drill continues until each player has returned to the starting positions.
4. The players may sprint either inside or outside the lines.
5. The coach, assistant coach, or managers may position themselves at each corner to be sure that players run outside of the lines. Chairs or other obstacles may also be used.

Teaching Points

1. Good power running from all players.
2. Reaction to signals from coach.
3. Players' heads up and alert at all times.
4. The competition factor: each player should work to his greatest potential. This drill, therefore, can be run by the players themselves as the season progresses.

Drill 2   Sprint, Stop, Pivot, Shuffle Drill

1. Players are lined up along the baseline.
2. Player 1 leaves the line and sprints to the position where the midcourt line and sideline intersect (meet). At this position player 1 comes to a two-foot (parallel) stop and reverse pivots on his inside foot (the foot closest to the center of the court). This is a 180-degree pivot, so that the player ends up facing the direction from which he began the drill.
3. Now player 1 shuffles on the midcourt line across to the opposite sideline, stops, reverse pivots on the outside foot (the foot closer to the sideline), and continues to shuffle to the corner where sideline and baseline meet. Player 1 continues the shuffle movement on the baseline, pivots again in the opposite corner, and moves to the halfcourt line. At halfcourt player 1 pivots again, shuffles across the midcourt line, and makes a final pivot before returning to the end of the line.
4. Players 2, 3, 4, and so on, delay their movement into the drill so that there is a proper interval between each player. They should delay until the player in front of them has pivoted at each position and started to move in another direction.

5. A coach may vary this drill by adding different movements. For example, players may sprint, stop, use the crossover step (instead of the pivot), or sprint again.

Teaching Points

1. Making a parallel stop with good balance.
2. Pivoting correctly.
3. Correct hand position and footwork when shuffling.

Drill 3 Sprint, Pivot, Shuffle, Run Backwards

1. Player 1 leads his teammates and sprints to midcourt, then pivots and shuffles to the baseline while facing the middle of the court. Player 1 touches the baseline, sprints to the foul line, and there turns and runs backwards down court to the starting position.
2. Players may run straight backward or in a zigzag pattern.
3. Players 2, 3, 4 and others move as described in Drill 2.
4. The number of times the players go through this drill will vary.

Teaching Points

1. Correct stop and pivot.
2. Running backwards with head up and hands ready.

Drill 4 Sprint, Stop, Sprint, Stop

1. Players are in line along the baseline facing midcourt (the number of players may vary).
2. On a signal from the coach, all players sprint to the foul-line extended area where they make a stop (either a stride or a parellel stop) before sprinting again to midcourt, three-quarter-court, and the opposite baseline.
3. After reaching the baseline, players pivot and return to their starting positions using the same procedure.
4. The coach may designate as many stops as he chooses or he may use a signal, such as a whistle, to cause the players to stop and start.
5. This drill may also be run sideline to sideline.

Teaching Points

1. Body should be low and on-balance when the stop is made.
2. The hands are kept in a ready position.

GROUP REACTION DRILLS

Drill 5   Change of Direction, Alertness Drill

1. Players are in line under the basket, behind the baseline.
2. Player 1 (on the signal) sprints to the midcourt line and touches the floor in the middle of the circle, runs backward to the foul line and there also touches the floor, and finally begins a defensive shuffle movement toward the right sideline. Once there, player 1 touches the right sideline and then shuffles across the court to the left sideline. He touches the sideline, shuffles back to the foul line, and then shuffles back to the baseline starting position where he is ready to go again.
3. Each remaining player will begin to move just as the player in front of him reaches the top of the foul circle. All players follow the lead of player 1.

Teaching Points

1. Talk and communication while moving at full speed. Knowing where each player is in relation to others.
2. Correct footwork and foot and hand positions.
3. Teamwork on defense concept.
4. Each player's knowledge of his position on the court.

Note: The following may be used as an alternate for Drill 5.

1. Place players in this drill in the same manner as Drill 5. (Exceptions will be in the final phases of the drill.)
2. The drill continues (as in Drill 5) until players reach the left sideline. Here the players will do a designated number of fingertip pushups or another exercise which a coach may choose (e.g., tipping, situps) and return to the starting position.
3. Also, as indicated in this figure, the players will pick up a ball, dribble the length of the floor to the far basket, take a layup shot, rebound their own shot, and dribble quickly back to place the ball in a designated area so that it is available for their teammates. Players then sprint to the beginning position ready to go again.

Teaching Points

1. Talk and communication while moving at full speed. Knowing where each player is in relation to others.
2. Correct footwork and foot and hand positions.
3. Teamwork on defense concept.
4. Each player's knowledge of his position on the court.

1 2 3 4 5

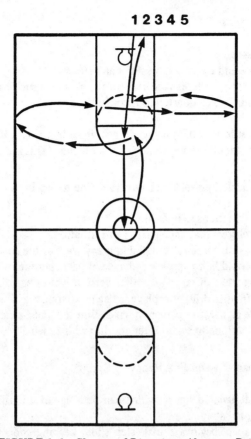

FIGURE 1-1   Change of Direction, Alertness Drill

5. Execution of pushups and other exercises.
6. Speed dribble and layup shot.

Drill 6   Suicide Sprints

1. Players are in line along and outside of the baseline. The numbers in the line may vary, with safety and spacing a major concern (one method may be to match up the team according to size and have the players of comparable size run with each other).
2. The players sprint to the foul-line area, touch the floor; sprint to the baseline, touch the floor; sprint to midcourt, touch the line, and return to the baseline; sprint to the opposite foul line-extended area, touch the floor, and return to the baseline; sprint to the opposite baseline, touch it, and return to the starting positions.
3. Variations of this drill are to sprint forward and run backwards, and to start by running full court (just the opposite of the basic drill).

Teaching Points

1. High speed.
2. Balance and footwork on starts and stops.
3. All these sprints can be run at any position such as one-quarter-court, halfcourt, three-quarter-court or full court.

Note: Be sure that the players do not finish by running into a wall or barrier and stopping their momentum with their hands. (This is a safety factor.)

Drill 7   Suicide Sprints Crosscourt (Sideline to Sideline)

1. Same directions as in Drill 6.
2. More players may take part in this situation.
3. Either drill can be alternated in many ways at the coach's discretion. One plan would be to employ a change of pace; in other words, a fast pace for a designated distance. Another version would be to have a whistle-stop drill. In this drill, the players begin to sprint, and as the coach gives a whistle signal, the players must assume a parallel-stride stop. The players then continue to sprint after another whistle signal.

Drill 8   Team Five-on-Five Recovery Sprint

1. On a designated signal, which can be a slap of the ball or a whistle, players immediately react.
2. All players begin a shuffle-step slide, keeping good body balance back toward midcourt and keeping eyes on ball or coach at all times.
3. As the players approach midcourt, another signal is given and all players sprint to defensive positions in free-throw lane.

Teaching Points

1. Reaction to whistle.
2. Shuffle-step movement.
3. Teaches transition from offense to defense.

Drill 9   Team Five-on-Five Sprint, Pivot, and Retreat

1. On designated signal, using a ball or whistle, players react immediately.
2. Pushing off foot closest to basket, after pivoting to face ball, players sprint to midcourt area.
3. Pivoting to face ball, they then retreat backwards to the free-throw area to assume defensive positions.

Teaching Points

1. Quickness.
2. Pivoting.
3. Ability to run backwards.
4. Knowing where the ball is at all times.

GROUP DRILLS WITH THE BALL

Drill 10 Team Five-Man Recovery
Sprint with Reaction to the Ball

1. As the players are retreating toward the foul-line area, as in Drill 9, the coach may pass or roll the ball in the direction of one of the players.
2. The players must have their heads up and be looking for the ball.
3. In this drill, the coach will have rolled the ball in the direction of players 5 and 3, who react toward the ball in an effort to gain possession. Player 5 gets the ball, recovers it, and may call "ball" to indicate to teammates that he has possession of the ball.
4. When the other team members see or hear the signal that player 5 has gained possession, they break quickly up the court, making the change from defense to offense.
5. Player 5 will pass quickly ahead to an open team member, in this example player 1, who in turn passes ahead to player 4. Player 4 drives in for a layup shot.
6. The players may run off the court to be replaced by another five who run the same drill, or the coach may have the first five continue to run the same drill again. The coach may also combine another drill with this drill—as in Drill 9.

Teaching Points

1. Quick transition from offense to defense and defense to offense.
2. Passing ahead quickly to an open teammate.

Drill 11 Team Five-Man Recovery
and Reaction—Continuity

1. Player 4 takes the ball out-of-bounds after making the layup shot.
2. Players 2 and 1, and 3 and 5, react quickly as the shot is made and break quickly to the sideline to be ready for the outlet pass from player 4. Players do not react to these positions until they see that the shot has been successful. If not, they rebound the missed shot until the score is

made; the player who scores the basket or a player designated by the coach takes the ball out-of-bounds and makes the pass in.

3. In this drill, player 4 passes to 2, who passes up court to 1, while players 5 and 3 move quickly to their positions on the opposite sideline.
4. Player 1 may pass immediately to player 5, or player 1 may dribble toward the basket and then pass.
5. The drill may end here or may continue back to the other basket in a particular manner designed by the coach. For example, the coach may direct the players to move quickly into their full-court zone pressing positions if the team is using this type of defense or have them retreat to a half-court defense position as indicated in Drill 10.

Teaching Points

1. Quick transition from offense to defense and defense to offense.
2. Passing ahead quickly to an open teammate.

Drill 12   Mirror or Gorilla Team Drill

1. A player in front of the group dictates all movement. Whatever moves that player makes, all other players make the same moves.
2. The drill has the players in defensive stance, heads up and ready, completing a lateral, frontwards, backwards, shuffle-step slide drill.
3. Other aspects of conditioning may be used by the coach in this drill such as hand quickness and running in place.

Teaching Points

1. Defensive footwork fundamentals.
2. Discipline and reaction (by watching for signals).
3. A tremendous conditioning drill.

Drill 13   Outline of the Court

1. Player 1 begins shuffle-step slide toward the corner of the court, in good defensive stance.
2. At the corner of the court, player 1 pivots on foot closest to the baseline and makes a quick turn to face into the court. Player 1 then continues to shuffle toward midcourt. Each player follows in the same manner.
3. At certain intervals along the outline of the court, the coach gives a signal, and all players perform designated conditioning drills such as running in place or jumping in place.
4. When reaching point B at the far end of the court, player 1 pivots on foot closest to the sideline and makes a quick turn facing into the court.

5. The drill continues around the full outline of the court until player 1 becomes last in the line.

Teaching Points

1. Footwork in defensive stance.
2. Keeping hands ready at all times.
3. Quick turns.

Drill 14   Baseball Pass—Two Players

1. The coach passes the ball to player 1. As the ball comes in, player 2 sprints down court, staying wide. The coach may also be positioned at halfcourt so that the pass must be thrown over the coach's head.
2. At the foul-line extended area, player 2 makes a sharp angle cut or loop toward the basket. Player 2 should have the inside hand up, giving a target to the passer, and should be looking for a pass.
3. Player 1 receives the pass from the coach, turns, and dribbles two or three times up court. At the moment of passing the ball, player 1 pushes off the back foot. In the pass, player 1 must follow through with the arm and hand so that the pass will be straight.
4. Player 2 receives the ball, drives toward the hoop, and drives for the layup.
5. After throwing the pass, player 1 sprints toward the basket to become the rebounder and must recover the ball before it touches the floor.
6. The same procedure occurs on the opposite side of the floor at the same time with players 3 and 4.

Teaching Points

1. Speed and quickness.
2. Passing the ball so that the receiver catches it in full stride and is able to remain under control.
3. Receiving the ball and shooting under control.
4. Playing both sides of the court.

Drill 15   Baseball Pass—Third Player on Defense

1. Players 2 and 3 perform the same procedures as the passer and receiver, players 1 and 2, in Drill 14.
2. Player 1 passes ball to player 2 and immediately begins to sprint to the other end of the court in a direct line to the basket. The purpose is defensive, that is, to deflect the pass and/or stop the receiver from scoring.
3. As in Drill 14, the passer will be the rebounder.
4. This drill is run on both sides of the court.

Teaching Points

1. Speed and quickness.
2. Passing.
3. Receiving the ball and shooting.
4. Playing both sides of the court.

Drill 16 Baseball Pass—Two Players in Continuous Action

1. The coach can pass the ball in or be near the midcourt to bother the pass. Players 1 and 2 will run the drill both ends of the court.
2. Player 1, the passer, performs the same procedure as in Drill 14. Player 2 also performs in the same manner as in Drill 14.
3. When shooting, player 2 turns and breaks again toward opposite basket. Player 1 rebounds, dribbles out, and throws another baseball pass.
4. Player 1 executes two baseball passes and rebounds twice. Player 2 shoots two layup shots. They then switch positions.

Teaching Points

1. Speed and quickness.
2. Passing.
3. Receiving the ball and shooting.
4. Playing both sides of the court.

Drill 17 Passing-on-the-Move Drill

1. The players are positioned as indicated. On both sides of the court, two lines are formed approximately ten feet apart. Both lines will run the drill full court both ways.
2. The players in both lines sprint at top speed, or, the shuffle-step/slide may be used in its place.
3. Player 1 gives a pass, which may be a two-hand chest pass or a one-hand push pass. Player 2 must have hands ready to receive the pass.
4. Player 2, upon receiving the pass, gives a return pass to player 1.
5. When players 1 and 2 reach the baseline, they push off the foot closest to the baseline and continue the drill to the other end of the court.

Teaching Points

1. Speed and quickness.
2. Footwork: shuffle; stops.
3. Hand-eye coordination.

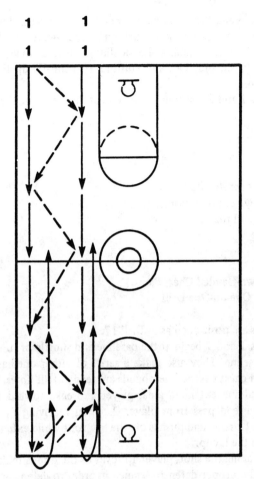

FIGURE 1-2 *Passing-on-the-Move Drill*

Drill 18 Passing-on-the-Move Drill

1. Players are positioned in two lines as indicated in Drill 17.
2. Player 1 runs to the outside of the sideline and continues to run this pattern to the baseline and around the court. When running, player 1 will be slightly ahead of player 2, who will run inside the court. Player 1 must have his hands ready to receive the ball. Upon receiving, player 1 gives a one-hand push pass or a two-hand chest pass to player 2 and continues running along the baseline up the other sideline.
3. Player 2 gives a one-hand push pass or a two-handed chest pass to player 1 and begins to shuffle to midcourt. While continuing to shuffle past midcourt, player 2 will receive and return passes with player 1.

4. When passing the foul-line extended area, player 2 slows, pivots with the foot that is closer to midcourt, and continues to shuffle facing the baseline. When approaching the sideline, player 2 slows, pivots on the foot closer to the sideline, and continues to shuffle up the court facing the sideline.
5. Players 1 and 2 continue to the end of the court and then switch positions.

Teaching Points

1. Speed.
2. Footwork: shuffle.
3. Hand-eye coordination.
4. Pivots and turns.
5. Passing.

Drill 19   Two-Handed Chest Pass, Layup, and One-on-One Drill

1. Players are positioned as in Drill 17.
2. Players 1 and 2 begin at the baseline and shuffle or run toward the opposite baseline. They also make a series of either one-handed push or two-handed chest passes. Their hands are ready at all times. When approaching the foul-line extended area, player 1 breaks toward the basket and receives a lead pass from player 2. Upon receiving a pass from player 2, player 1 drives and pushes off the left foot while extending the right arm to take the layup.
3. After taking the shot, player 1 moves to the opposite side of the court and takes the proper defensive stance in order to defend against player 2 in a zigzag movement down the court to the baseline.
4. After player 1's layup, player 2 rebounds the ball, dribbles to the opposite side of the court, and from there proceeds to dribble up the court in a zigzag fashion. Player 2 uses the crossover dribble so that both hands will be alternately drilled. This procedure is followed until players 1 and 2 reach the opposite baseline. They then switch positions and move to the end of the lines.

Teaching Points

1. Quickness.
2. Receiving a pass and shooting while on the move.
3. Defensive footwork.
4. Dribbling against pressure defense.

Drill 20   Four-Post Cutting and Passing Drill

1. Players 2, 3, 4, and 5 are positioned near the edge of the circle above the foul line. Players 5 and 3 are facing their teammates who are at the base-line. Players 2 and 4 face in the direction of the opposite baseline, ready to receive passes from the cutters when they return to the other end of the court.
2. Players 1, 6, 7, 8, 9, 10, 11, and 12 have a ball (if there are enough balls available).
3. Player 1 passes to 5, using a two-hand chest pass (or any other pass desig-nated by the coach), and cuts quickly toward halfcourt ready to receive a return pass from player 5. Player 5 returns the ball to player 1 who passes quickly, without dribbling, to player 3. After making this pass,

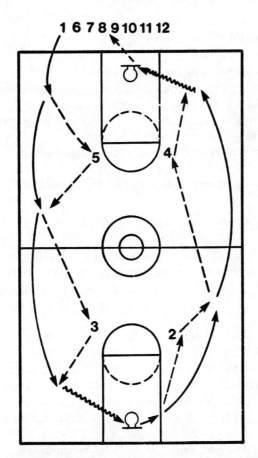

FIGURE 1-3   *Four-Post Cutting and Passing Drill*

player 1 cuts up court and toward the basket, ready for a return pass from player 3. Player 1 receives the pass from 3 (a soft flip pass or hand-off) and drives to the basket for a layup shot. Player 1 rebounds the shot, passes quickly to 2, cuts up court for a return pass, passes to 4, and cuts past 4 for a return pass and then the layup at the other end.

4. Player 1 rebounds the shot and hands the ball to a teammate who may not have a ball.
5. The players following 1 do not make their passes and cuts until the player in front of them receives the return pass from the first post man (player 5).
6. The drill may continue by having the players switch to the left side immediately or repeat the movements on the same side more than once. After each player has gone through the designated routine, four new players replace 2, 3, 4, and 5 at the post positions. Players 2, 3, 4, and 5 now move into the passing-cutting line.

Teaching Points

1. Strong wrist passes by the cutters.
2. Hard drive and cut up court for the return pass and layup.
3. No dribble will be used unless going for the layup.
4. Hands must be in the ready position at all times, and post players should also be ready to step and meet the passes.
5. The post player should make soft, easy-to-handle return passes to the cutters.
6. Emphasis on making the layup after a high-speed drive.

Drill 21   Six-Post Cutting and Passing Drill

1. Players 7, 9, 10, and 12 are positioned at the foul-line extended area, about three feet in from the sideline, with their backs to it.
2. Players 8 and 11 are positioned at the edge of the center circle.
3. Players 1, 2, 3, 4, 5, and 6 are positioned along the baseline; each player has a ball.
4. Player 1 passes to player 7, cuts up court and receives a return pass from 7; 1 then passes to 8, cuts and receives a return pass from 8; 1 then passes to 9, cuts, receives a return pass from 9, and drives to the basket for a layup. Player 1 recovers the ball from the basket and returns up the court, using the same procedure in passing to players 10, 11, and 12.
5. Player 2 and succeeding players do not begin until the player in front of them has passed to the post player at midcourt.
6. As in the four-post drill, this drill may be repeated on each side and for as many times as the coach may designate.

Teaching Points

1. Handling and passing the ball on the move.
2. Not dribbling except when making a drive to the basket for a layup.

Drill 22 Perfect Drill—Continuous Action

1. Player 5 is positioned in the lane ready to take the ball out of the basket, step out-of-bounds, and make a pass to player 1. Players 3 and 4 are positioned at the foul-line extended area about three feet from the sideline. Player 1 is near the top of the circle, ready to move to the ball side, and player 2 is near the top of the circle at the other end of the court in a diagonal position from player 1.

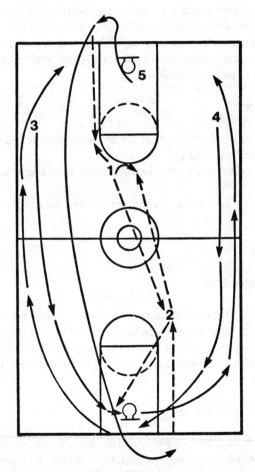

FIGURE 1-4 *Perfect Drill—Continuous Action*

2. As player 5 steps out-of-bounds ready to pass, players 3 and 4 start running up the sideline toward the opposite basket (A). Player 1 moves to his left to receive player 5's pass.

3. Player 5 passes to 1 and sprints up court to recover the shot taken by player 3 before the ball hits the floor (B). Player 5 steps out-of-bounds and passes to player 2 to start the action going the other way, while players 3 and 4 cross over to the opposite sideline and sprint up court to continue the drill.

4. After passing to player 2, player 5 sprints up court to try to recover the ball before it hits the floor after the shot by either player 3 or 4.

5. After receiving player 5's pass, player 2 passes quickly to player 1, who in turn looks to pass to either player 3 or 4 for the layup shot.

6. The drill continues for a specific number of trips up and down the floor or until a pass is dropped, a dribble is taken, or a shot is missed.

7. When the first group does not complete the drill "perfectly," they are replaced by a second group and must come back to do it again.

8. The positions of the players may change each time the drill is run, with a major emphasis being that all players, big and small, must be able to sprint baseline to baseline continuously.

Teaching Points

1. Movement by players to meet the ball with good body position and hands ready (players 1 and 2).

2. Players' movement to fill the lanes every time a lane in front of them is open.

3. The importance of hustle, conditioning, and the basics of the layup shot.

STATION DRILLS

Drill 23   Station Drills

The purpose of these drills is manifold: first, to teach the concept of conditioning, and secondly, that of self-discipline and hard work. Stations are also a very efficient way of conditioning a team, especially in the early stages of the season. The gym area is divided into different positions; at each position a drill is conducted with a basic goal in mind.

23a Pegboard or Chalkboard

This board can be placed on any wall; for example, over the door to the locker room. The board will have different heights, to be marked with pegs or chalk. Each day the players work on their jumping ability. Players should each jump as high as they can, extending their arms and placing a peg in a hole in the board, or marking the board with chalk. The purpose of this drill is to improve players' jumping each day, each week.

23b Jump Rope

At another station, the coach can have any number of players working on jump ropes. All players should jump on their toes. The coach can designate this to be done in a repetitive series of jumps, in a total number, or in a net time period. This is a drill that the coach makes progressively more difficult.

23c Bench Jump

The next position can be set up using any number of benches and players. Each player assumes a position next to the bench. Upon the designated signal, each player crouches, jumps over the bench, and so on back and forth across the bench to the end. Again this drill can be used in many ways, such as those mentioned in the previous drill.

23d Tipping Drill

This drill positions a player facing the basket or the wall. The player tips the ball off the board or wall repeatedly, using fingertips, first with the right hand, then the left hand. The second part of the drill involves three players who weave continually following one another to tip the ball to the board. This drill teaches teamwork; it is also a great conditioning drill.

23e Passing Against the Wall

The coach stations six players in a line facing the wall, each with a ball. At a designated signal, the first player races toward a point. As the players run, they give a two-handed chest pass or one-handed push pass off the wall slightly ahead of them. Hands must be ready at all times. The other five players continue the drill in succession. As each player reaches the final designated position, he races back to the beginning to continue the drill.

23f Big-Man Drill

Two players are positioned at the free-throw line with their backs to the basket. The drill begins at the coach's signal: the players turn and race to the basket. As they approach the basket, they assume a crouched position, jump up, and touch the backboard with both hands as high as they can. After touching the board, the players race back to the free-throw line, touch the floor, then race back to the backboard. This is done six times; after a ten-second rest period, they execute another series. This is an extremely difficult but very effective conditioning drill.

23g Mikan Drill

The coach can set a player at each available basket. Each player has a ball standing directly in front of the basket. On the designated signal, the players begin by taking a short hook layup with the right hand, catching the ball before it hits the floor. Then each player takes a layup shot with the left hand. The drill can be conducted by a total number of baskets, or by a set time. The drill can be done in alternate sequence by using a power layup move, a jump shot drill, or a reverse layup drill.

23h Rebounding

Mention must be made here of the use of a rebounding machine. There are various methods and drills with it which result in a general buildup of endurance and stamina.

Teaching Points

1. These drills can be run in a series, and in any form or set pattern at the coach's discretion.
2. The drills should be implemented at the beginning of each practice. They should be alternated each day to avoid a monotonous routine.
3. These drills can be used off-season, along with roadwork and other drills.

2

Passing Drills

INTRODUCTION

Scoring is the ultimate goal of basketball, but passing is the fundamental move leading to the scoring attempt. No player can expect to score continually through his or her own effort. The skill of passing is most important for all players at every level of competition.

First of all, in order to become a good passer, a player must develop good basketball hands. This means the fingers, wrist action, and follow-through play an important part in passing.

Secondly, a player who learns to pass ahead to an open player is an invaluable asset to any team. Combining a sense of when to pass with the proper form of how to pass leads to successful teams.

Coaches should emphasize quickness in passing and remind the players that their hands should always be ready to receive the ball. Coaches, when teaching passing, should stress and repeat the following phrases: come to meet the pass; give a target to the passer; watch the ball into your hands; pass quickly; and keep two hands on the ball.

A player will gain more by handling the ball slowly at first, developing skills and confidence, and gradually working into more difficult drills. This chapter deals with drills that are, by design, progressive. It begins with drills of a fundamental nature and moves up to the level of competition in game-like situations at top speed. The types of passes used by a player and the team are at the discretion of the individual coach.

THREE-OR-MORE-PLAYER DRILLS

Drill 1 Two-Ball Quickness Passing and Receiving Drill

1. The team may be divided into groups of three and placed in position at the four corners of the halfcourt area.
2. Each group has two balls (here player 1 and player 3 have a ball) and they pass quickly to player 2 and to each other. Player 1 passes to 2, and just as he releases his pass, player 3 passes to 1. Player 1 quickly returns the pass to 3 and prepares to receive a pass from 2, who will make this pass just as 1 releases the ball. Players 2 and 3 continue to alternate passes back and forth to player 1 and should try to time their passes so that they will not pass to 1 while he still has a ball in his possession.
3. The players rotate to the player-1 position at the coach's signal.

Teaching Points

1. Correct hand position. The hands of all the players should be ready to receive the ball at all times.
2. Quick release of the ball. As each player receives the ball, he is ready to pass the ball back immediately. There should be a good follow-through as well.
3. Hand and eye coordination.

Drill 2 Two Lines—Stationary Drill

1. The players are positioned opposite each other about ten feet apart in two lines which extend from the free-throw line to midcourt.
2. The coach is positioned so that he may watch each player in order to check that each player uses the correct form when passing (e.g., two-handed chest pass).
3. Player 1 passes to player 2, who will pass to player 3. The drill continues until the ball has reached player 12.
4. The coach moves in the same direction as the ball so that he may watch each pass very closely and make corrections when needed.
5. After the ball has reached player 12, it will be passed back to player 11 and to 10 and so on until it reaches player 1. The coach will move backward as he observes each passer.

Teaching Points

1. Foot and hand positions of the passer and receiver.
2. The proper wrist action when making the pass so that there is good follow-through, guaranteeing good controlled passes.
3. Stepping to meet the pass as well as stepping with the pass as the player makes it.
4. Concentration by the receiver as he "watches the ball into his hands."

**Drill 3   Handoff Drill or Soft
Pass Drill (Also Underhand)**

1. Players are positioned in two lines facing each other in an area between the top of the key and midcourt. The first players in each line are ten to fifteen feet apart.
2. Player 1 passes to player 2 and moves quickly to the end of line 2. Player 2 passes to the second player in line 1 and moves to the end of line 1. After passing the ball, each player steps to the left (or right) so that there will not be a collision or a breakdown during the drill.
3. The movement continues for a predetermined period of time (e.g., thirty seconds, one minute) and the speed or tempo of the drill may be changed by a signal from the coach.

Teaching Points

1. The passes from player to player should be quick but soft and easy to handle. The coach should stress moving to meet the ball, as well as stepping toward the receiver when passing.
2. Players should not allow the ball to touch the floor.
3. The handoff or flip pass is made at waist level and can be made with one or two hands. The passer should not jam or force the ball into the hands of the receiver but should try to let the ball "hang in the air" and be taken and controlled by the receiver.

Drill 4   Follow-the-Leader Passing

1. Players are positioned in two lines at the baseline and on either side of the foul lane. The first player in each line has a ball in his possession.
2. Player 1 dribbles away from the line toward midcourt. After taking four or five quick dribbles, player 1 stops and turns so that he may pass to player 2, who is ready to move and receive the pass.
3. The pass may be a hook pass, underhand pass, or any pass designated by the coach. After passing, player 1 runs quickly to the end of the line.
4. Player 2 receives the pass, dribbles, stops, and makes the same pass to player 3. All players will follow the same procedure.

5. When player 1 returns to the front of the line, he continues the drill but changes the type of pass.

Teaching Points

1. The coach should stress the correct execution of each pass as well as teach the correct method of picking the ball up after a player has stopped the dribble.
2. The proper dribbling, stop, and turn techniques must be observed carefully and corrections should be made on the spot.

Drill 5   Quick-Passing Drill
With Coach in the Middle

1. The players are positioned either in two lines facing each other or in a semicircle. The coach is positioned in front of and at the center of the semicircle or between the two lines.
2. The coach becomes actively involved in this drill as he moves forward and backward between the lines and makes a series of quick passes to the players, who are in a ready position.
3. As the ball is passed from player to coach and back again, the coach will make blind passes or fake one way and pass the other way. The purpose here is to emphasize that the players should be alert and ready to receive the ball at all times.
4. After a series of passes, the players should rotate positions.

Teaching Points

1. Emphasize the alertness of each player while watching the coach and the ball.
2. The hands of the players should be always in the ready position.
3. This drill is designed to help each player to understand that good, quick passes do not have to be hard passes which the receiver will have problems handling.

Drill 6   Peripheral Vision
Two-Ball Passing (Six Players)

1. Five players are positioned from one wing position, across the free-throw line to the other wing. Player 6 faces the other players. Players 6 and 1 each have a ball in their possession.
2. Player 6 passes to 2. As soon as player 6 releases his pass to 2, player 1 passes to 6. Player 6 quickly passes to 3 and prepares to receive a return pass from 2.

3. The drill continues in the same manner, as 6 passes to 4 and 5 and then returns, down and up the line for a designated period of time. After the designated time period, the players alternate positions until each player has taken a turn at being in front of the group.

Teaching Points

1. Player 6 remains in a stationary position and uses peripheral vision to follow the flight of each ball.
2. The players in the line do not pass to player 6 while 6 has a ball in his possession.
3. Players are to pass quickly but are in the drill to help one another.
4. The point is to try to see the ball out of the corners of the eyes rather than focus complete attention on the ball.
5. Emphasize that players should be in a good stance, not standing up straight. Players' hands should be in a position ready to receive the ball at all times.
6. Emphasize the idea of players helping each other with good, timely passes.
7. Introduce the competitive idea as to who can be the player to last the longest in the drill.

Drill 7 Peripheral Vision and Quickness
Passing—Four Players, Two Balls

1. Same positioning and activity as in the previous drill, with three players instead of five positioned near the free-throw-line area.
2. Emphasize the same fundamentals as in Drill 6.

Drill 8 Bull in the Ring

1. Five players are positioned at the outer edges of the free-throw circle.
2. One player, player 6, is positioned in the center of the circle prepared to play defense.
3. The players on the perimeter of the circle will pass to each other, while player 6 will defend against the passes and try to intercept or deflect the ball.
4. The offensive players should pass the ball quickly but are not permitted to pass to the player who is on their immediate left or right. The movement continues until player 6 either intercepts or deflects the ball. The player who makes the bad pass changes position with player 6.
5. Another method for making the change of players would be to allow the defensive player to remain in that position for a specified amount of time (for example, 30 seconds). The players would alternate every 30 seconds until such time as each player has taken a turn in the middle.

Teaching Points

1. Stress short, quick passes. The players should release the ball quickly and keep their hands always ready to receive the ball.
2. Players should fake the passes to try to force the defensive player to move.
3. The defensive player should use the proper hand position and foot movements.

TEAM DRILLS

Drill 9 Four Corners—Pass and Follow (Chest Pass with One Ball)

1. The players are positioned in four lines.
2. The ball is in the possession of player 1 (as the players improve their skills, a second or third ball may be added), who will start the drill after a signal by the coach.
3. Player 1 passes to player 2, who steps to meet the pass. Player 1 sprints quickly to the end of line 2 after passing, while player 2 turns or pivots toward line 3 and passes to player 3. Player 2 sprints to the end of line 3, and player 3 passes to 4, and 4 to 1, as the drill continues.
4. The direction of the ball may be reversed on the coach's signal.
5. The passes may also be varied at a signal from the coach.

Teaching Points

1. Players should use a quick wrist release when making the pass and should step in the direction of the pass.
2. Stress moving to meet all passes and the importance of stepping up to the ball so as to place one's body between the ball and the defensive player.
3. The passer should concentrate on passing the ball to a particular area, such as the chest level of the receiver, and the receiver should act as a good target, away from an imaginary defensive player.

Drill 10 Four Corners—Pass and Follow and Receive a Return Pass

1. The players are positioned in four lines at each corner of the halfcourt area.
2. At first the ball is in the possession of player 1 (a second ball may be added as skills are developed).
3. Player 1 passes to player 2 and cuts directly toward him or her so that player 1 may receive a return underhand flip pass from 2. Player 2 then

cuts toward line 3 and receives a short return pass (two-hand chest or one-hand push pass) from player 1, who moves quickly to the end of line 2.
4. Player 2 passes to player 3, receives a return pass from 3, and then passes again to 3 who starts his cut toward line 4. Player 2 then moves to the end of line 3. The drill continues in this manner until the players have returned to their starting positions.
5. The direction of the ball may be reversed on the coach's signal.

Teaching Points

1. Handling the ball with speed and accuracy while on the move.
2. Making a "soft" pass to a cutter moving toward the passer and passing quickly to the player cutting away from the player with the ball.
3. Keeping the hands ready and above the waist at all times.

Drill 11 Four Corners—Chest
or Bounce Pass with Pivot

1. The players are positioned in four lines at each corner of the halfcourt area.
2. Player 1 passes, using a bounce pass, to player 2, who steps to meet the pass. Player 2 catches the ball while on the move, then stops and pivots on his right foot and steps in the direction of line 3. (The pivot may be either a reverse or front pivot.) Player 1 sprints to the end of line 2 after passing to player 2.
3. Player 3 steps toward 2 and receives the pass. Player 3 pivots and passes to player 4. The drill continues in the same direction and then may be reversed.

Teaching Points

1. Receiving the pass while moving forward. The coach should also emphasize the passer should deliver the ball so that it will be received in a position where it may be easily handled.
2. Correctly executing the stop and pivot. The coach must stress coming to a correct parallel or stride stop and pivoting away from the defensive player. The player receiving the ball should be ready, in a crouched position, when making his stop. The hands should be kept ready above the waist to receive a pass.

Drill 12 Pass and Replace Drill

1. The players are positioned in two lines which stretch across the court from sideline to sideline and are about fifteen to eighteen feet apart. Two other players stand between the two lines (numbered 5 and 6 in this drill).

2. Player 1 starts the drill by making a pass to player 6 and then follows his pass and replaces player 6.
3. Player 6 may pass in any direction to any player. For example, he passes to player 10 and replaces him. Player 10 passes to player 7 and replaces him. Player 7 passes to player 5 and replaces him.
4. The drill may continue for a period of time or for a designated number of passes, or until stopped by the coach.

Teaching Points

1. The ball may be passed to any player, so all players must be in position prepared to receive the ball.
2. The coach should emphasize the fundamentals of passing.

Drill 13   Wall Passing

1. The coach may place a number of markings on the wall of the gymnasium (for example, +'s). All marks may be at the same height or at different heights with the height being determined by the kind of pass being practiced. The coach may also use a ball-toss machine if he has one available.
2. Each player has a ball and is positioned in front of one of the wall markings. Players then will pass the ball a predetermined number of times (e.g., 30, 40, or 50) or will pass for a designated period of time (e.g., 30 seconds or one minute).

Teaching Points

1. Emphasize having the correct form when making the pass. Players should pass with a good follow-through motion.
2. Stress the correct foot position.
3. There must be quickness when making the pass.

Drill 14   Two-Players, One-
Ball Passing Drill—Chest Pass

1. The team or group is divided into pairs and positioned at intervals around the full court with the players about twelve to fifteen feet apart.
2. The players pass to each other for a prescribed period of time (30 seconds, 60 seconds).
3. All types of passes may also be practiced in this drill. The drill is designed for the players to work on fundamentals and to help each other.

Teaching Points

1. Correct passing form and technique with a quick release and follow through.

2. Correct hand position when receiving a pass.
3. Stepping to meet a pass (step toward the passer).
4. Stepping with the pass (step toward the receiver as the pass is made).

Drill 15 Baseball Pass, Overhead Pass, and Bounce Pass Drill

1. The players are positioned as in Drill 14 but are about fifteen to eighteen feet apart.
2. The various passes mentioned in the title of the drill are practiced for a prescribed time.

Teaching Points

1. Correct passing technique.
2. Proper reception of the pass.
3. Stepping with each pass as it is made and stepping to meet the pass when receiving it.
4. Giving the passer a target. That is, the receiver indicates, by extending his hand to the side, the location to which he wants the pass to be thrown.

Drill 16 Bounce Pass and Chest Pass Combination Drill with a Defensive Player (2 on 1)

1. The players are positioned in such a manner that the two offensive players are about twelve feet apart and facing each other. The coach can set up six sets of three players in the halfcourt area or anywhere on the court.
2. The defensive player is positioned midway between players 1 and 2 and will attempt to intercept or deflect a pass being made from 1 to 2, or from 2 to 1. If X is successful in deflecting, intercepting, or forcing a bad pass, he is replaced in the middle by the player making the bad pass.
3. Players 1 and 2 are restricted in their movement. Each player is allowed to make a one-step pivot in any direction when making the pass. The receiver must also have the same restriction but should be ready to move to go after any bad pass.

Teaching Points

1. Quick passing with the use of fakes by the offensive players.
2. Aggressive action by the defense including the bluff-and-drop technique.

Drill 17 Pass and Cut—No Dribble Until the Layup Shot

1. The players are positioned as indicated, with all players in line 1 in possession of a ball.

2. Player 1 passes to player 2, runs up the court, and receives a return pass from 2. Player 1 passes quickly to player 3 at midcourt and continues to cut up court ready for a return pass from 3. Player 1 passes quickly to player 4 and cuts to the basket for a return pass and a layup shot. Player 1 retrieves the rebound, passes to player 2, and makes a return to the starting position by using the same procedure as the move up court.
3. The second and succeeding players will follow player 1 after he has made his pass to player 4 and will continue the drill until each player has moved up the full court. The line will then move to the left side and complete the drill.
4. After completing the drill, the cutters change positions with the receivers.

Teaching Points

1. The passes used may be varied according to the directions of the coach.
2. Stress quick release of the passes and strong cuts to the basket.
3. There is no dribbling in this drill, except on the approach to the layup shot.

Drill 18 Multipass Drill

1. The players are positioned as indicated and player 1 has a ball in his possession.
2. Player 1 starts the movement by passing to player 2, who is stepping to meet the pass. This first pass by 1 is a two-hand chest pass (A). After passing to player 2, player 1 fakes and cuts to the outside of 2, ready to receive a handoff pass from player 2 (B).

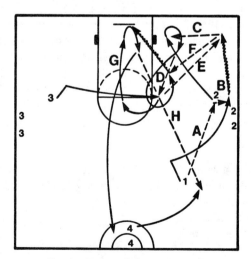

FIGURE 2-1 Multipass Drill

3. After the handoff, player 1 dribbles toward the corner and player 2 pivots and cuts toward the basket. Player 1 stops his dribble and throws a hook pass (C) to player 2, who has cut toward the block of the foul lane (as indicated in the diagram). Player 2 receives the ball while on the move, stops, and makes a reverse pivot so that he may make a bounce pass (D) to player 3, who has cut from the opposite wing position to a position at the edge of the foul lane. Player 3 times his cut in a manner that allows him to arrive at his position to receive player 2's bounce pass while still moving.

4. Player 3 makes a one-hand push pass (E) to player 1, who has held his or her position after making the hook pass to 2. This pass by player 3 is made immediately after gaining possession of the ball.

5. After passing to player 3, player 2 cuts inside the foul lane as he or she follows the pass in the direction of 3, and circles player 3 in such a manner that he or she is ready to receive a bounce pass or underhand shovel pass from player 1 (F). Player 2 will receive this pass while on the move and drive to the basket for a layup shot.

6. As soon as player 3 sees that player 2 has received the bounce pass from 1 and is making a drive toward the basket, player 3 moves to a rebound position in the middle of the lane (G). Player 3 rebounds player 2's shot and makes a baseball pass or two-hand overhead pass (H) to player 4, who has moved to the outlet area indicated in the diagram.

7. Player 1 moves to line 2, player 2 moves to line 3, player 3 moves to line 4, and player 4 moves to the 1 position.

Teaching Points

1. The coach should stress moving to meet the ball and catching the ball while moving.
2. The coach should also emphasize the fundamentals of all types of passes.

Drill 19   Five-Point or Star-Passing Drill

1. The players are positioned as indicated, with player 1 in possession of the ball.
2. Player 1 passes to player 4 (A) and runs quickly to the end of line 4. Player 4 passes to player 3 (B) and runs to the end of line 3. Player 3 passes to 2 (C); 2 passes to 5 (D). The drill continues until all players have handled the ball a designated number of times.
3. The drill may be run with only five players or with five lines of players.

Teaching Points

1. There must be quick, accurate chest or one-hand push passes.
2. Each player runs to the line to which he made the pass.

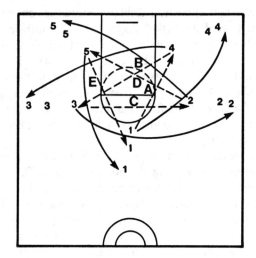

FIGURE 2-2 Five-Point or Star-Passing Drill

3. To make the drill effective there must be continual movement by all players.

Drill 20 Quick Passing

1. Players are positioned in two lines near the midcourt line.
2. Each pair of players will have possession of a ball.
3. Player 1 passes to player 2, who is moving toward the baseline, and player 1 then moves toward the baseline. Player 2 returns the pass to player 1 and continues to move.
4. The players exchange as many passes as possible before reaching the baseline and then return to their starting positions by making a series of passes near the sideline.

Teaching Points

1. Players should make as many passes as possible while moving at high speed.
2. Coach must stress to the players to keep their hands ready and to make quick return passes.

Drill 21 Baseball or Lead-Pass Drill

1. The players are positioned in two lines as indicated. Each player in line 1 has a ball.

2. Player 1 dribbles toward the sideline and stops about 8 to 10 feet from the sideline. Player 2 follows player 1 and then cuts to the outside and toward the basket, looking for a lead pass from player 1.

3. Player 1 passes to player 2, using a lead pass that will be taken in full stride, as he cuts to the basket.

4. The coach is positioned between the passer and receiver so that he forces the passer to make an accurate loop pass over his head.

5. After passing, player 1 retrieves the rebound of player 2's shot. Player 1 runs out-of-bounds and then makes a baseball pass to player 2, who breaks to the sideline opposite the side from which he shot. After passing to 2, player 1 sprints to the end of line 2 while player 2 dribbles to line 1. The drill continues as the players switch lines and sides.

Teaching Point

1. Stress the accurate lead pass to the cutter so that the ball may be handled easily.

Drill 22   Pass-and-Follow
Drill—Mix the Passes

1. The players are positioned in four lines as shown in the diagram, with player 1 in possession of the ball.

2. Player 1 passes to player 2 using a baseball pass (A). Player 3 cuts toward

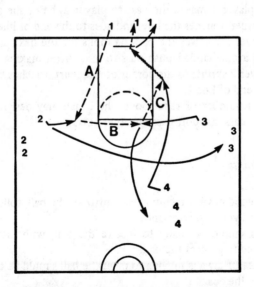

FIGURE 2-3   Pass-and-Follow Drill—Mix the Passes

the foul line as player 1 passes to 2. Player 2 passes to player 3 using a two-hand chest pass (B).

3. As player 3 receives the pass from 2, player 4 fakes and cuts toward the basket and receives a bounce pass from 3. Player 4 shoots a layup shot, retrieves the rebound or makes a basket, and passes to the next player in line 1.

4. Player 1 moves to line 2, player 2 moves to line 3, player 3 moves to line 4, and player 4 moves to line 1.

Teaching Points

1. The drill is designed to stress moving to meet passes and passing on time to the receivers.
2. Players should work on the timing of their cuts toward the ball.
3. Proper execution of the various passes should be emphasized.

Drill 23   Corner Passing Drill

1. Two lines are positioned in this way: line 1 is in the right corner at mid-court near the hash mark, and line 2 is on the left side of the court about five feet in from the sideline at the foul-line extended area.
2. One ball is used; line 1 begins the drill by giving a chest (two-handed) pass to the first player in line 2, who runs to meet the pass.
3. After player 1 makes the pass to player 2, he or she sprints to the baseline corner, touches the line, and goes to the end of line 2.
4. As player 2 receives the ball, he looks for the next player in line 1 and makes a one-handed push pass to him. After making the pass to player 1, player 2 sprints to the corner of midcourt, touches the line, and moves to the end of line 1.
5. After a number of repetitions, the coach may designate the use of the bounce pass, handoff pass, or other passes.

Teaching Points

1. Stress good passing techniques, control of the ball, follow-through on the pass, and good body balance.
2. Players should be ready to receive the ball, with their hands and arms extended to protect the ball.
3. The idea of always moving to meet the ball should be constantly encouraged by the coach.
4. Sprint or cut hard and fast after passing.

COMPETITIVE DRILLS

Drill 24   Three-on-Two Passing Drill

1. Player 1 begins the drill at the top of the key. Players 2 and 3 start in positions between the free-throw line extended area and the baseline. Players X1 and X2 are in defensive positions in the lane.
2. Player 1 passes to either side. As the defense drops off, player 1 goes to the free-throw line and toward the ball.
3. Player 2 gives a return pass to player 1 and goes to the block at the low-pivot area.
4. Player 1 gives a quick pass to the weak side to player 3, who should be moving toward the block at the low-pivot area. Player 1 remains at the foul-line area but covers his pass (moves toward the side he passes to).
5. If player 3 does not have a layup shot, he looks to the weak side for player 2.
6. There should be a shot after three or four passes.
7. After a shot, the three players rotate lines. Player 1 becomes 3, player 2 becomes 1, and player 3 becomes 2. Defense stays on until they work against three groups.

Teaching Points

1. Stress good passing techniques.
2. There should be constant movement. Players should move to a new area after making a pass so that they may create passing lanes.

FIGURE 2-4   Three-on-Two Passing Drill

3. Players should always look to the weak side on offense if they have no shot.
4. Power layup moves should be used once the offensive players receive a pass in a position close to the basket.
5. The tandem defense work must be aggressive, and the players must hustle at all times as they try to prevent any easy shot or a rebound after a miss.

Drill 25   Triangle Passing Drill

1. The players are positioned in three lines.
2. The purpose of the drill is use all types of passes to get the ball to the forward and pivot areas for a layup.
3. Player 1 is at the guard position to the right of the free-throw line. Player 2 is at the forward position between the free-throw line extended area and the baseline. Player 3 is in the low-pivot area. Players X1, X2, X3 are in defensive positions.
4. Player 1 gives a pass to player 2. As player 2 makes a target for the pass, the foot and leg nearest the defender are extended to block out the defensive player so that the reception can be made. As player 2 receives the ball, he should be low and have good body balance.
5. Player 2 pivots to face the basket and looks into the pivot area in order to pass to player 3. If the defense plays with his arms and hands high, player 2 should fake and pass near the hip of the defender. If the defender's hands are kept low, player 2 should fake and pass close to the defender's ear.
6. Player 3 works for position and with the defense on his back, tries to keep the body between the ball and the defender. If player 3 cannot

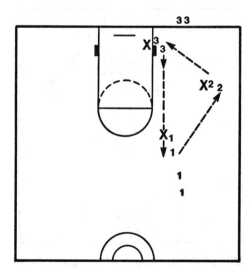

FIGURE 2-5   Triangle Passing Drill

make a move to the basket, then pass back to the forward or the guard, and the drill continues.

Teaching Points

1. Stress passing techniques to be used from different positions.
2. Quick, short passes should be used.
3. Players must move to get into a better position to receive the ball.

Drill 26 Pass and Pivot

1. The players are positioned in two lines with the first player in line 1 in possession of the ball. Line 1 sets up to the left (or right) of midcourt with the first player located about five feet from the hash mark. Line 2 is positioned to the left of the foul lane with the first player set up about five feet from the sideline at the foul-line extended area. (More than one group of players may be positioned in different parts of the court for this drill.)
2. The first player in line 1 passes to the first player in line 2 (A), who steps to meet the pass so that he receives the ball while he is moving. After passing, player 1 sprints to the end of the opposite line.
3. After player 2 receives the pass, he or she stops, makes a reverse pivot, and passes (B) to the next player in line 2, player 4, who is ready to step to meet the pass. After making this pass, player 2 sprints to the end of the opposite line.
4. The drill continues with the next pass (C) being made to the second player in line 1, player 3, who meets the pass, pivots, and passes (D) to player 5. The drill continues with player 5 passing to player 6, cutting to the end of the opposite line, and passing to player 2, who has moved to be the first player in the opposite line.

Teaching Points

1. Emphasize stopping and pivoting after having caught the ball while moving.
2. Players should concentrate on making perfect passes to the receiver who is moving.

Drill 27 Four-Corner Baseball Pass

1. The players are positioned in four lines in each of the corners of the court. The first players in lines 1 and 2, which are on the same side of the court, have a ball in their possession.
2. The drill begins with players 1 and 2 making a baseball pass to the line in the opposite corner. Player 1 passes to player 3 and player 2 passes to

player 4; after passing, players cut and sprint to the end of the line to their right (in this diagram, player 1 moves to line 2, and player 2 moves to line 3).

3. Players 3 and 4, after receiving a pass from players 1 and 2, will in turn make a baseball pass back to the next player in the line from which the pass to them was made. Player 3 passes to line 1 and sprints to the end of line 4; player 4 passes to player 2 and sprints to the end of line 1.

Teaching Points

1. Emphasize the techniques of the baseball pass, which must be thrown a long distance. The players should know that the ball will curve when thrown a long distance and that the correct hand and wrist action should be used when making this pass.
2. The receiver must be alert and ready to move to receive this pass.

3

Dribbling Drills

INTRODUCTION

This chapter is devoted to the development of dribbling skills. Dribbling is an individual skill and has an important place in basketball.

The dribbling technique that should be taught to beginning players at all levels involves the fingertips, which control the ball; the wrist, which gives the force and pushing motion that places the ball on the floor; and the forearm of the dribbling hand, which performs in a pumping fashion. The upper arm stays very close to the dribbler's body, while the forearm forms about a forty-five-degree angle away from the player's side. The ball is pushed to the floor by combining each of these parts—the fingers, wrists, and forearm work together to maintain a firm, steady rhythm.

The dribble can be an asset to any team, provided it is used to the best possible advantage. It should not be permitted to ruin team movement and team play. A good rule to follow is to always have a purpose in mind, either to drive directly toward the basket or to give a fellow player a scoring opportunity.

The ball should not be dribbled unless the player will be thereby improving his position on the court. Also, players should be taught not to stop or pick up their dribbles until they have a teammate to pass to or are in a position to shoot. A player should always be alive with the ball and never pick the ball up with nothing to do but hold it.

The following drills are progressive, beginning at the most basic level and moving up to the more difficult levels which include the use of the dribble in team offenses.

INDIVIDUAL DRILLS

Drill 1   Wave Dribble Drill

1. The players are spread out between midcourt and the baseline, leaving enough room for each to move freely.
2. Knees should be bent with good body balance. The wrists are kept firm with the fingers spread wide to control the ball.
3. The coach stands directly in front of the players and gives directions to the players to move laterally, forward, and so on.
4. The players should protect the ball with their bodies and their free hand.
5. On the last signal, the players speed-dribble to the opposite end of the court and then back to their starting positions.

Teaching Points

1. Players should use a good dribble protection position.
2. Each player should have his head up and should use the slide dribble as he simulates looking for a teammate to pass to.
3. On the speed dribble, stress pushing the ball out in front so that the player will be able to attain maximum speed.

Drill 2   Stationary Protection Drill

1. Four lines are in position facing the coach. The lines extend across the foul lane from sideline to sideline.
2. The first player in each line has a ball. Each player begins to dribble in a stationary position.
3. At the coach's signal, usually the raising of a hand, the players must change their dribbling hand. As each player changes dribbling hands, he remains in the same stationary position.
4. The dribbler will use a dribbling maneuver designated by the coach.

Teaching Points

1. Dribblers should stay in good low position.
2. Nondribbling hands and arms are kept in protecting positions.
3. The players' eyes should be on the coach.
4. The change of hands should be done quickly by keeping the ball low and pushing it across the front of the body to the free hand, which is in a

position to receive the ball as the transfer is made. The free hand must be in the ready position so that the transfer can occur without a fumble taking place.

HALFCOURT DRILLS

Drill 3 Zig-Zag Drill

1. The players are positioned in two lines at the baseline, one on each side of the court between the lane and sideline.
2. Players 1 and 2 begin to dribble up court with their right hand. After five or six dribbles, at a controlled pace, the players push the ball from their right to their left hand. As the players push off their left foot they cross their right leg over to protect the ball. They continue up the court in the same manner until they reach the halfcourt line.
3. After five or six more dribbles, the procedure is continued with the players' left hand pushing the ball to their right hand. When the players reach the baseline they turn and continue the drill back to the starting positions and give the ball to the next player in line.
4. As the players' skills become better, the coach can add the reverse dribble, the fake-reverse dribble, or the change-of-pace dribble.
5. A defensive player can be added later so that two skills can be practiced in one drill.

Teaching Points

1. Using correct dribbling technique with either hand, on both sides of the court.
2. Dribbling at varying speeds.
3. Using various types of dribbles.
4. When the defense is added, having good footwork and correct use of the hands.

Drill 4 Dribble Tag Drill

1. Ten players are involved. Eight are stationed around the jump circle. Players 1 and 2 are inside the circle.
2. All ten players have a ball, if possible. Players 1 and 2 are designated as "it." The coach signals the beginning of the game.
3. Players 1 and 2 attempt to tag the other players, who will avoid the tag by dribbling away. They must keep one hand in the air as they begin to try to tag another player.
4. The other players may dribble anywhere in the halfcourt area to prevent

being tagged. Once a player is tagged, he becomes "it" and goes to the center of the drill.

5. A variation of this drill is to have each player who is tagged leave the court and see how long it takes one or two dribblers to tag everyone.

Teaching Points

1. Players must keep their eyes off the ball and their heads up as they dribble.
2. Players must use the full-speed dribble, change-of-pace dribble, and all other maneuvers to prevent being tagged.
3. The restricted area helps to develop quickness while dribbling.

Drill 5 Four-Line Drill

1. Four lines of players are positioned at the baseline, with the first player in line in possession of a ball. At the coach's signal (e.g., a clap of hands or a whistle) the players begin to dribble in control, concentrating on fundamentals.
2. On the coach's next signal, the players make a crossover dribble. This maneuver is done with three repetitions before reaching midcourt, where players come to a parallel stop, pivot, and resume the drill back to the baseline.
3. On their next turns, players will use a reverse dribble, fake-reverse dribble, or other type.
4. As the players finish one series they rotate to the next line to their left or they may go to the end of the same line.

Teaching Points

1. Using correct protection dribbling techniques.
2. Keeping the eyes up, and looking for the hand signals.
3. Maintaining concentration and the use of both hands.

Drill 6 Control, Speed and Weak-Hand Dribbling Drill

1. Players are positioned in three lines at the baseline with the first player in each line in possession of a ball.
2. Each player uses good body balance, with the foot opposite the dribbling hand slightly forward and with his body protecting the ball.
3. Players use a control dribble and periodically work on change-of-pace, crossover dribbles, and so forth until reaching midcourt.
4. At midcourt, each player uses a speed dribble, using the best hand or the weak hand, and races to the baseline. After reaching the baseline the player pivots, pushes off the back foot, and goes upcourt again.

5. Upon completion of the drill, players rotate to the line on their left or go to the end of their own line.

Teaching Points

1. Concentration on dribbling techniques.
2. Emphasis on the use of the weak hand in the speed dribble as the players advance in their ability to use both hands.
3. Emphasis on protecting the ball in all parts of the drill.
4. Individual competition as well as team competition (these can be put into the drill as the skills progress).

FULL COURT DRILLS

Drill 7 Full Court Sideline Drill

1. Players are positioned in two lines at the baseline at the corners of the lane.
2. Player 1 begins to speed-dribble with the left hand on the inside of the court up to the midcourt line, where he or she will use a crossover dribble.
3. As player 1 starts, player 2 begins the same routine on the outside of the court but uses his left hand.
4. With a quick burst, both players continue to the baseline corner, where they come to a stop, pivot on their back foot, and reverse the ball to the other hand; then they speed-dribble to the next baseline corner where they perform another reverse-dribble move.
5. Players 1 and 2 then proceed to the midcourt line to perform a crossover dribble.
6. The drill is completed with a speed dribble to the baseline, another reverse dribble, and then a handoff to the next player in line. Players go to the end of the other line after giving the handoff.

Teaching Points

1. Stress that the eyes should be up and looking ahead while the body protects the ball during the reverse movement.
2. Stress dribbling techniques in the crossover and reverse moves. Players should not leave the ball exposed as the reverse is made.
3. Stress the use of both hands when making the reverse dribble and also the correct reception of the ball with the free hand as the transfer is made.

Drill 8   Dribble Tag

1. The team may be divided into groups of four, five, six, or seven players with each player having a ball; for example, two groups of five players at each end of the court.
2. One player is designated as "it" in a game of tag. The player must tag another player while continuing to control his dribble. The other players must also control their dribble while trying to avoid being tagged.
3. The players must stay within certain boundary lines; for example, using half of the main court. Also, the players may be restricted to using only their left or right hands, or they may use both hands at the direction of the coach.

Teaching Points

1. Players keep their heads up while dribbling.
2. Quick stops, starts, and changes of direction should be made. The use of the slide dribble is emphasized in this drill especially when players are attempting to avoid a tag.

Drill 9   Speed Dribble Race

1. There are four lines of players, two at each end of the court behind the baseline on each side of the foul lane.
2. Players 1 and 2 begin a speed dribble up the court, on the coach's signal.
3. As they approach players 3 and 4 at the opposite baseline, they come to a two-foot stop and give a good handoff pass. Players 3 and 4 continue the speed dribble to the other end and hand off to the next player in lines 1 and 2.
4. The point of completion of the drill is to be designated by the coach; for example, when the players return to starting positions.

Teaching Points

1. Each player must push or keep the ball out in front.
2. Stress the use of both hands—the right hand going up from number 1 and 2 positions, the left hand from number 3 and 4 positions.
3. Emphasize concentration of all aspects of the drill, especially coming to a stop and making a good pass.
4. As the season progresses, try to instill the aspect of competition into the drill.

Drill 10   Dribble Race—Down and Back

1. Players are placed in two lines at the baseline on each side of the lane. Each line has a ball.

2. At the coach's signal, players 1 and 2 begin to speed-dribble to the other end of the court and across the baseline. Without stopping, the players return back down the court and hand off to the next player in their line.
3. The players may alternate hands, or the drill may be run again with players using only their right hand or left hand.
4. The "game" is won by the line that finishes first.

Teaching Points

1. Keeping the ball out in front while dribbling at great speeds.
2. Making a good handoff pass to assure the next person (teammate) that he will be able to start his dribble correctly and not lose time.
3. Engaging in competition.

Drill 11 Pass, Follow, and Dribble Drill

1. Players are stationed in two lines at the baseline on each side of the lane. The first player in each line sprints to the edge of the foul lane, pivots, and faces player 2.
2. Player 2, who has possession of a ball, gives a two-hand chest pass to player 1, just as player 1 makes a pivot.
3. Player 2 fakes and follows the pass. A return pass is given to player 2 on either side by player 1.
4. When player 2 receives the ball, the drill continues with a speed dribble to the opposite end of the court. Player 1 follows player 2 to the other end of the court and rebounds or gains possession of the made shot.
5. After the layup shot, the players dribble the ball up the sideline and move to the end of the line.

Teaching Points

1. Good passing techniques for the chest pass and handoff. The cutter should also fake before moving to receive a return pass.
2. Speed dribbling techniques.
3. Correct layup shooting form at the end of the speed dribble. Emphasize slowing down and gaining control of the ball with both hands.

Drill 12 Dribble, Stop, and Handoff to the Trailer

1. The players are positioned in three lines at one end of the court at the baseline.
2. The player in the middle (2) has a ball and, using a control dribble, dribbles toward one side or the other.
3. Approximately halfway between the free-throw line and the midcourt line, player 2 stops, pivots on the inside foot or on the foot closest to the

center of the court, and hands off to the next player, who fakes and times the cut.

4. Player 1, who receives the ball, now dribbles with the left hand through midcourt toward the opposite sideline; stops, pivots on the inside foot, and hands the ball off to the next player, who has been moving down court at a controlled pace in the far outside lane.

5. Player 3 dribbles past the top of the basket key area to a point at the free-throw line extended area. Player 3 stops, pivots on the inside foot, and hands the ball off to player 2, who fakes to the outside, comes inside to receive the ball, and breaks in for a layup.

6. Player 1 rebounds, players 2 and 3 fill the lanes, and the drill continues back down court in the same manner. After the shot is taken and the ball is recovered, the next three players run the same drill.

Teaching Points

1. Emphasize good dribbling techniques—stay low, protect the ball, and keep eyes and head up.
2. Stress good handoff and passing techniques after making a good pivot.
3. Players should fill the lanes and time their cuts and fakes before they make the move to the ball.
4. Players should use the weak hand when dribbling.
5. Players should learn layup shooting technique.

PROTECTION DRIBBLE DRILLS

Drill 13   Dribbling Protection and
Speed-Dribble Race with Obstacles

1. The players are positioned in two lines at the baseline. The first player in each line has a ball. Three chairs (or obstacles) are placed on each side of the lane and are spaced about ten feet apart between the foul-line extended area and midcourt.

2. On a signal from the coach, the players with the ball dribble quickly to and around the first chair, keeping their bodies between the chair and the ball. (The players in line 1 start to dribble with the left hand, and the players in line 2 dribble with the right hand.) The dribbler continues around the second and third chairs. After circling all the chairs, the dribbler uses a speed dribble back to the starting position and passes, using a good handoff, to the next player in line.

3. Each player takes a turn, with the team finishing first declared the winner.

4. After the first "game," the teams change sides so that each will have had a turn using their left and right hands.

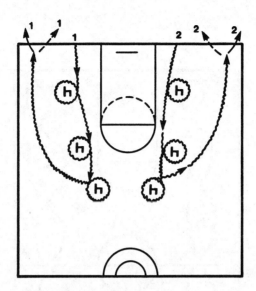

FIGURE 3-1 *Dribbling Protection and Speed-Dribble Race With Obstacles*

Teaching Points

1. Stress keeping the body between the ball and the chair.
2. Players should make a proper stop and handoff after returning to the starting position.

**Drill 14   Obstacle Dribble—Players Dribble at
Each Other; Emphasize Keeping Their Heads Up**

1. Chairs or obstacles are placed at intervals over the full length of the court.
2. The players are positioned in four lines, two at each end of the court on the baseline on either side of the lane.
3. On the coach's signal, the first player in each line begins to dribble. The players are to use a weaving motion, dribbling in and around the obstacles using crossover dribbling techniques.
4. The players must react when they approach another player coming toward them. One player must go inside and the other player go to the outside.

Teaching Points

1. Stress dribbling fundamentals.
2. Emphasize keeping the head up with eyes off the ball and on obstacles and other players.
3. Have players use various types of dribbles in the drill.
4. Emphasize working together in all aspects of the drill.

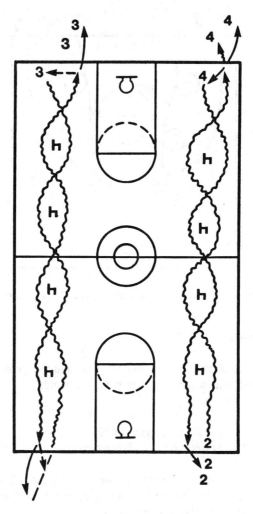

FIGURE 3-2   Obstacle Dribble—Players Dribble at Each Other; Emphasize Keeping Their Heads Up

Drill 15   Crossover Dribble Through
Chairs or Obstacles—Full Court

1. The players are positioned in two lines behind the baseline on either side of the foul lane. The first player in each line has a ball (or all players have a ball if there are enough available).
2. Four chairs (obstacles) are placed in positions extending from the foul-line extended area to the hash mark in the front court.
3. The first player in each line dribbles toward the chairs and uses the

crossover dribble to move past the chairs. After reaching and circling the last obstacle, the player speed-dribbles back to the starting position and gives the ball to the next player in line.

Teaching Points

1. Players should stay in a low, balanced position with knees flexed.
2. Emphasize using the body to protect the ball as the crossover is made.
3. Stress correct crossover techniques.
4. This drill may be used as a team race or as a race against the clock.

Drill 16 Protection Dribble Around Chairs or Other Obstacles

1. Obstacles (e.g., chairs) are placed at spaced intervals over the full length of the court.
2. The players are in two lines, one on the right side, the other on the left, at one end of the court.
3. Players in both lines dribble simultaneously toward the first obstacle and proceed to dribble around it while protecting the ball.
4. As the players finish circling the last obstacle, they go to the outside of the court and speed-dribble to the end of the line; they then proceed to the end of the opposite line.

Teaching Points

1. Stress correct form when using the protection dribble.
2. When circling the obstacle, players should keep their head up, eyes off the ball, and their body between the obstacle and the ball.
3. This drill may be run as a team race or as a race against the clock.

Drill 17 Weave and Layup Drill

1. The coach may use any number of obstacles for this drill. The obstacles can be chairs, cones, or players. Both sides of the floor may be used, with the players moving in opposite ways for safety purposes.
2. Four lines of players are in position, two at each end of the court.
3. As the players reach an obstacle, they use the dribble designated by the coach to go around it. Players may use the change-of-pace, crossover, reverse, or fake-reverse dribbles.
4. As the players go around the last obstacle, they dribble hard to the basket for the layup shot. They retrieve the ball, hand it to the next player on their side of the court, and go to the end of the line.

Teaching Points

1. Good dribbling techniques.
2. Use of both hands.
3. Use of both sides of the court.
4. Layup shots.

DRIBBLE AND DRIVE

Drill 18   Crossover and Reverse Dribble

1. Players are positioned in two lines, one at midcourt and one on each side of the lane. The coaches are positioned on either side of the foul lane at the foul-line extended area.
2. The first player in each line begins dribbling straight toward the baseline. Each player approaches the free-throw-line extended area, where the coach is positioned, and pushes the ball from one hand over to the other, crossing the front leg over to protect the ball.
3. After breaking in for a layup shot, the player retrieves the ball, passes it to the next player in the opposite line, and moves to the end of that line.
4. Players use the reverse dribble in the next repetition of the drill.

Teaching Points

1. Correct dribbling techniques with emphasis on the first quick step that is made after changing direction.
2. Layup shots.

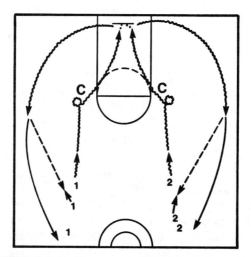

FIGURE 3–3   Crossover and Reverse-Dribble Drill

Drill 19 Two-Foot Stop and Pivot

1. Three lines are positioned at the baseline with the first player in each line having a ball.
2. At the coach's signal, players 1, 2, and 3 begin to dribble. At a point parallel to the foul line, or on the coach's signal, the players come to a two-foot stop so that they can reverse-pivot in either direction.
3. At a signal, the players pivot right or left and make a pass back to the next player in line.
4. After passing the ball, the players go to the end of the line and prepare to go again.

Teaching Points

1. Dribbling with either hand.
2. Making a two-foot stop (parallel) with good balance so that the pivot can be made.
3. Using the essentials of good passes to the next man in line.

Drill 20 Stopping—Parallel and Stride Stop

1. Players are positioned in five lines. The player at the front of each line has a ball.
2. Each player dribbles to a point parallel to the foul line, stops with both feet side by side, keeping his body on balance and ready to pass. The players continue to the midcourt line and stop in a stride position (one foot in front of the other), ready to pass. The players pivot and then continue the procedure back to the baseline.
3. After passing, the players go to the end of the line.

Teaching Points

1. Improving the fundamentals of dribbling and picking the ball up properly when coming to the stop.
2. Using correct footwork when stopping so that the body remains on balance.

STOPPING AND PIVOTING-OFF DRIBBLE

Drill 21 Stopping and Pivoting

1. The team is divided into two lines.
2. The players at the front of each line have a ball.
3. Player 1 dribbles quickly toward midcourt but is forced to come to a quick stop as Player X1 moves into his path. Player 1 pivots away from

X1's attempts to steal the ball from him. Player 1 may pass back to the next player in the line or may look to pass to the post man on his side of the court.
4. The players exchange lines after the pass: player 1 goes to X1 and X1 goes to 1. The ball is returned to the next player in line.

Teaching Points

1. Stopping on balance and under control.
2. Pivoting away from defensive pressure.
3. Accurate passing.
4. Keeping the head up and eyes off the ball when dribbling.

Drill 22   Dribble, Stop, Pivot, Cut, Handoff

1. Two lines are positioned at the baseline. The first player in each line has a ball.
2. Players 1 and 2 begin to dribble up court, followed by the second player in the line.
3. At a designated point or on a signal, the dribbler stops, pivots, and hands off to the second player, who cuts beside the dribbler for the pass.
4. The second player dribbles down court to another position, stops, pivots, and hands off to the first passer, who is cutting behind him.
5. After reaching the baseline, each player turns and continues the drill back toward the starting position and then gives the ball to the next player in line.

Teaching Points

1. Good dribbling techniques and proper timing of the cuts for the handoff.
2. Fundamentals of stopping and pivoting.
3. Teamwork—players should work together to help each other.

Drill 23   Dribble, Stop, Pivot, and Pass

1. The players are divided into four lines as indicated. The first player in lines 1 and 3 has a ball.
2. Players 1 and 3 dribble to the midcourt circle. Using a two-foot stop or a stride stop, players 1 and 3 pivot and pass to the next player. Player 1 passes to player 4; player 3 passes to player 2.
3. After a pass, each player goes to the next line to the right or to the line to which he passed.
4. Various types of dribbles may be employed in this drill.

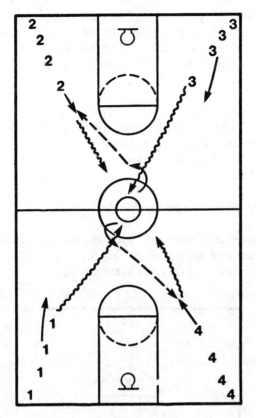

FIGURE 3-4 Dribble, Stop, Pivot, and Pass Drill

Teaching Points

1. Using proper techniques of dribbling and coming to an on-balance stop.
2. Making good passes to the next player in line, who should be ready to receive the pass.

COMBINATION DRIBBLING DRILLS

Drill 24 One-on-One Protection Dribble Drill

1. Two players are positioned in the free-throw circle.
2. Offensive player 1 takes a good dribbling position, with eyes up and off the ball and with the body protecting the ball.
3. Defensive player X1 must be in good defensive stance. The player must

use finesse, not power, to deflect the ball from the offensive player. If the defensive player does deflect the ball, the player moves to the offense.
4. The players must stay in the free-throw circle. A timekeeper determines the completion of the drill if the defense cannot take the ball away.

Teaching Points

1. Dribbling techniques, ball control, and body protection.
2. Good defensive stance and footwork.
3. Correct use of hands on defense.
4. Aggressiveness.

Drill 25   One on One—Using the Dribble

1. The players are divided into pairs and each player has a ball. They are positioned near the top of the key with one player designated as the offensive player and the other as the defender.

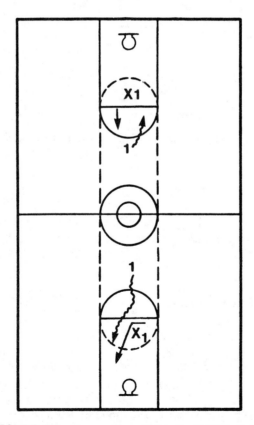

FIGURE 3–5 *One on One—Using the Dribble Drill*

2. Both players start to dribble while standing in place. Player 1 will try to dribble past player X1 so that player 1 can get free for a layup shot. Player X1 must try to get into position to prevent player 1's drive.
3. The players are restricted by the boundary lines which are the width of the foul lane apart and which extend from the baseline to midcourt. To force the action and prevent the defensive player from "sitting back," player X1 must try to knock away or deflect player 1's dribble. Player 1 must also use the same technique in order to get free.

Teaching Points

1. Quick fakes and changes of direction; also, change of pace.
2. Defensive footwork and body balance.

Drill 26   Circle Dribbling

1. The players are positioned in a line along the baseline. Each player has a ball (or as many players as possible).
2. Player 1 dribbles to the first circle, using the right hand, and moves around the circle. After completing the first circle, player 1 dribbles to the middle circle and repeats the move. Player 1 then moves to the third circle, dribbles around it, and shoots a layup.
3. After shooting, player 1 recovers the rebound and dribbles back to the starting line, using the same procedure.
4. The second player starts his movement just as the first player completes the first circle. The following players continue, using the same rules.
5. This drill may also be run with two lines at opposite ends of the court. They dribble toward each other from opposite directions and dribble around each circle.

Teaching Points

1. Use the protection dribble and keep the body between the circles and the ball.
2. Keep the head up so that collisions will be avoided.
3. Players may use the same hand or may alternate hands.

Drill 27   Two-Ball Dribbling Drill

1. Three lines are positioned behind the baseline at one end of the court. The first player in each line has two balls in his possession.
2. At a pace designated by the coach, players 1, 2, and 3 dribble both balls the length of the court and back again to the starting position.
3. The first player gives the balls to the next player in line, who continues the drill.

Teaching Points

1. Stress concentration on dribbling both balls simultaneously.
2. Have the dribbler try to keep the head up and eyes off the ball.

4

Shooting Drills

INTRODUCTION

This chapter deals with individual shooting fundamentals. The drills are repetitive and progressive: repetitive because there is continual emphasis on the basic mechanics of shooting and progressive because the sequence of drills goes from the layup shot to the jump shot, from drills at various positions on the court, and from individual-technique shooting drills to the use of those drills in the team system.

Although individual practice is necessary and beneficial, the best results are gained when players practice as often as possible in game-like situations. This can be accomplished through controlled, competitive drills.

The coach should stress the following points in teaching the fundamental aspects of shooting. First the player should maintain body balance, and secondly, the player should be squared off to the basket. The player's whole body, not just the face, must be square to the basket. Thirdly, the player's delivery should be stressed. The player should extend the shooting arm to a position where the ball is in front of and above the shooting shoulder. Finally, the term concentration should be stressed when instructing the shooter so that he or she will learn to select a particular spot on, inside, or over the rim and try to shoot the ball at that target.

There is a definite need for the drills throughout the year and for the continuous stressing of the fundamentals. Some players will develop the skills faster than others, but the idea of repetition must be established.

INDIVIDUAL DRILLS

Drill 1 Layup Drill—The Coach
Makes the Pass to the Shooter

1. One line is formed on either side of the court at a wing position. The coach is stationed in the foul lane near the foul line with the ball.
2. The first player in line fakes and cuts toward the basket with hands up and in position to receive the pass.
3. After receiving the ball, player 1 shoots a layup shot off the board.
4. After the shot, player 1 retrieves the ball and passes to the coach, who in turn passes to player 2, breaking to the basket.
5. After passing to the coach, the players move to the opposite side of the floor in order to continue the drill from that side.

Teaching Points

1. Layup-shot fundamentals should be stressed, such as moving off from the inside foot and lifting the knee toward the basket.
2. The coach should stress taking the shot off the backboard because it is a better percentage shot.
3. The cutter's hands should be ready to receive the ball, the cutter's eyes ready, always knowing where the ball is.
4. The coach should show the importance of the use of both hands and run the drill from both sides of the court.

Drill 2 One-Line Layup Drill

1. One line is positioned between midcourt and the top of the key about five feet in from the sideline. If possible, every player should have a ball.
2. Player 1 dribbles with the right hand toward the basket. As player 1 approaches the takeoff position, he or she lifts the ball with both hands and pushes off the left foot. Player 1 extends the right arm, laying the ball off the square on the backboard.
3. After the layup shot, each player retrieves the ball before it hits the floor, dribbles to the opposite side of the floor, and waits there until the last player has finished. The same procedure continues from the left side, with the players using their left hand.
4. An alternate to this drill is to move the players to each corner where they can practice shooting from the baseline angle. For example, if the players drive from the right corner, they use the left hand to shoot the layup. If they drive from the left side of the court, they use the right hand.

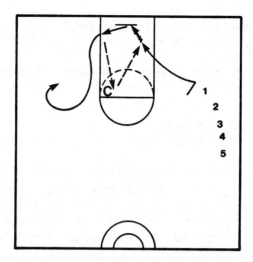

FIGURE 4-1 Layup Drill—The Coach Makes the Pass to the Shooter

Teaching Points

1. Dribbling methods and the correct procedure for lifting the ball into shooting position.
2. Correct layup shooting techniques.
3. Reacting quickly to recover the ball after the shot and not allowing the ball to hit the floor.

HALFCOURT DRILLS

Drill 3 One-Line Layup and Feed

1. The players are positioned as in Drill 2. Player 1 begins the drill by dribbling in to the basket and taking a layup shot.
2. As player 1 retrieves and gains definite possession of the ball, player 2 breaks to the basket ready to receive a pass from player 1.
3. Player 1 should give a good two-handed chest pass (a two-handed flip pass or a one-handed push pass) to player 2. After passing, player 1 goes to the opposite side of the court to continue the drill from that side. Player 2 proceeds to move in for a layup shot, retrieves the ball, turns, and passes to player 3, who is moving to the ball.

Teaching Points

1. Good layup-shot techniques must be emphasized by the coach.
2. Players should make a strong movement toward the basket on all shots.

3. Good passes to feed for the layup shot are of the utmost importance. The passer should make a quick but soft pass to the player who is moving toward him.
4. The coach should stress perfection in making perfect passes and in making all the layup shots.

Drill 4 Six-Basket Competitive Drill (Clock or Total Basket)

1. Three players are in a line at each basket, and each line has a ball.
2. The first player in each line dribbles in for a layup shot, retrieves the ball, and passes the ball to the next player in line. After making the pass to the second player in the line, the first player goes to the opposite side of the floor to start a line on that side and continues the drill after receiving the pass from player 3.
3. The drill may be timed or total baskets (ten) may be counted to win the game.

Teaching Points

1. Stress layups; shooting fundamentals must be constantly drilled.
2. Quickness should be emphasized. Players are to drive as quickly as possible to the basket.
3. The coach can establish competition among the players by putting the drill into game-like conditions.

Drill 5 Two-Line Layup Drill

1. Two lines are positioned on each side of the court with the same number of players in each line. Player 1 begins the drill by dribbling and shooting a right-hand layup shot off the board.
2. As player 1 dribbles toward the basket, the first player in line 2 moves in to retrieve the ball. As the rebounder gains control of the ball, player 2 breaks from the shooting line toward the basket. Player 1 has his arms and hands ready to receive the pass for the shot.
3. As the shot is being taken, the next player in line 2 moves to the basket to retrieve the ball and continues the drill by passing to the next player in the shooting line.
4. As each player shoots or passes to the next player, he moves to the opposite line.
5. Run the drill from the right repeatedly until twenty (or a specified number of) consecutive layups are scored, and then switch to the left side.
6. An alternate drill is to have the players release the shot on the opposite side of the basket for a reverse layup.

Teaching Points

1. Stress perfection and concentration. The players should not be lazy on shots and passes.
2. The cutter moves to meet the ball with the hands ready above the waist at all times.
3. The importance of following the shot and not allowing the ball to hit the floor should be stressed.

Drill 6 Two Lines—Partners Layup Drill— Circle, Dribble, Pass, Shoot

1. The players are positioned in two lines on the same side of the floor at the foul-line extended area. Each pair of players has a ball with the players in the line closer to the top of the key in possession of the ball.
2. Player 2 cuts toward the basket as player 1 dribbles toward the basket. Player 1 passes to player 2, who shoots a layup shot. Player 1 rebounds and passes to player 2 at the opposite wing position, who dribbles out to midcourt and joins line 1. Player 1 follows his pass to player 2 and goes to line 2.
3. The next pairs of players follow just as the preceding pair gain control or rebound the made or missed shot.

Teaching Points

1. Players should be in continuous movement, emphasizing correct timing on their drives to the basket.

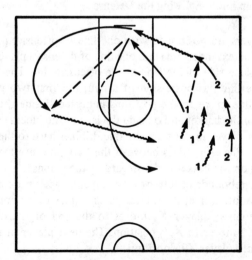

FIGURE 4-2 *Two Lines—Partners Layup Drill—Circle, Dribble, Pass, Shoot*

2. The correct timing of the pass to the cutter is one of the key points of the drill.
3. The correct execution of the layup shot should be stressed at all times, and players should constantly be reminded to concentrate on making this shot.

Drill 7   Two Lines–Layup Drill

1. Two lines are positioned on each side of the lane at the edge of the free-throw line. Line 1 is on the right side of the lane, and line 2 is on the left side.
2. The drill begins with the first player in line 1 passing to the first player in line 2, who fakes toward the baseline and cuts toward the pass. After receiving the pass, player 2 pivots and dribbles to the basket for a layup shot.
3. Player 1 follows the shot by player 2, retrieves the ball, and passes to the next player in the passing line.
4. Player 2 goes to line 1, and player 1 goes to line 2.

Teaching Points

1. Movement to meet the ball with the player's hands ready should be emphasized.
2. Stress layup-shot fundamentals when the player makes a hard drive to the basket.

Drill 8   Layup Shot–Splitting the Defense

1. The players are positioned with one line of offensive players at the free-throw line extended area and one line of defensive players at the baseline on the same side of the lane as the offensive line. The first player in the offensive line has possession of a ball; the first two players in the defensive line move to the positions indicated—inside the lane about four feet from the basket and outside the lane at the block.
2. The first player in the offensive line dribbles hard to the basket for a layup shot. Player 1 drives between the two defensive men, while keeping the eyes on the basket and disregarding the defense.
3. Player 1 rebounds or retrieves the ball and passes back to the next player in the shooting line; then, after passing, goes to the end of the defensive line. Defensive player X1 moves to the end of the offensive line and player X2 moves to X1's position. The next player in the defensive line moves into player X2's position.

Teaching Points

1. Emphasize making the layup shot under pressure and concentrating on the target. The driver should think only of making the shot and then react to the movements of the defense.
2. The defensive players must attempt to bother the shooter in any way possible, with the exception of making a serious foul that will prevent the shot from being taken.

Drill 9 Three Lines—Straight-Lane Cutting for the Layup

1. Three lines are positioned at midcourt with players 2 and 3 near the left and right sidelines and player 1 in the midcourt circle with a ball.
2. With the lanes moving straight up court, player 1 passes to player 3, receives a return pass, and, while on the move, gives a pass to player 2 on the opposite wing.
3. Player 2 returns a pass to player 1, who stops at the free-throw line, fakes, and passes to player 3 for a layup shot.
4. Player 2 rebounds and passes to either player 1 or 3, who have both moved to the outlet positions. The player who receives the outlet pass should make a quick pass to the next player in line 1, who continues the drill by passing to player 3 or 2.
5. The players change lines: player 1 moves to line 3, player 3 moves to line 2, and player 2 moves to line 1.

Teaching Points

1. Emphasize passing and receiving on the move with the hands kept ready at all times.
2. Stress the use of correct layup shot techniques.
3. Emphasize that keeping the lanes wide makes it more difficult for the defense to play the break.

Drill 10 Three-Lines Halfcourt Weave Drill

1. Three lines are positioned at midcourt. Players 2 and 3 stand wide of each sideline, while player 1 is at the midcourt circle in possession of a ball.
2. Player 1 passes to player 3 who makes an angle cut toward the middle of the court. Player 2 cuts behind player 3 after making the pass and continues toward the basket.

3. Player 3 passes to player 2 who cuts toward the top of the key area. Player 3 cuts behind player 2 and continues toward the basket.
4. Player 2 dribbles to the free-throw line, fakes one way, and passes the opposite way to player 1, who goes in for a layup shot.
5. After passing, player 2 goes to the outlet position on the side to which he passed, and player 1 moves to the outlet position on the other side. Player 3 rebounds and gives an outlet pass to player 1, who makes a pass to the next player in the midde line at midcourt.
6. The next three players continue the drill; the players who have completed the drill move to the end of a different line: player 1 moves to line 3, player 3 moves to line 2, and player 2 moves to line 1.

Teaching Points

1. Players should receive the ball on the move in a position to be able to pass, dribble, or shoot. Stress that the passer should make a pass that is easy to handle.
2. Emphasize the fundamentals of the layup shot, especially lifting the ball to shooting position and releasing the shot the correct distance from the basket. The player should not leave his feet too early or too late.
3. Emphasize shooting from both sides of the floor.
4. Players should make a strong, accurate outlet pass after rebounding or after stepping out-of-bounds with the ball following a made shot. The outlet pass receiver should always be ready to step to meet the pass.

Drill 11   Four-Corner Layup

1. Two lines of players (1 and 2) are positioned at the guard positions to the left and right of the foul circle. Two more lines (3 and 4) are positioned in the left and right baseline corners, and one line (5) is positioned under the basket with the first player in possession of a ball. Player 5 will begin the drill.
2. Player 5 passes to player 2, who is moving to meet the pass, and after making this pass, player 5 sprints to the end of line 2. Player 2 should receive the pass near the foul-line extended area.
3. Player 2 now passes to the first player in line 3 and sprints to the end of line 3. As player 3 receives this pass, player 4 starts a cut toward the ball and is ready to receive a pass from player 3. Player 3 passes to 4 and sprints to the end of line 4.
4. Player 4 passes or hands off the ball to player 1, who cuts toward the basket and drives in for a layup. After passing to player 1, player 4 sprints to the end of line 1. The shooter moves to the end of line 5, and the next

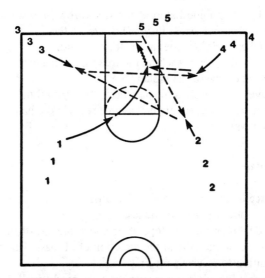

FIGURE 4–3 Four-Corner Layup Drill

player in line 5 recovers the made shot and continues the drill by passing to line 2.

5. The drill may continue until a specific number of layups have been made.

Teaching Points

1. Emphasize moving to meet all passes with the hands in a ready position.
2. Quick passes should be made and players must handle the ball on the move. Constant movement allows all players to get into the flow of the action.
3. Stress the necessity of concentration when making the layup shot.

FULL COURT DRILLS

Drill 12 Three-Line
Full Court Layup Drill

1. Players are positioned in three lines at the baseline on both ends of the court.
2. Player 1 is in the middle with the ball, and players 2 and 3 fill the outside lanes close to the sidelines.
3. Player 1 begins the drill by giving a two-handed pass to player 3. Player 3 immediately returns the pass to player 1 and continues up court. Player 1 gives a pass to player 2, who returns it to player 1.

4. Player 1 makes a good stop at the free-throw line, stays low, and passes to either player 2 or 3. Player 1 stays at the free-throw line until the shot is taken and then goes in for the rebound.
5. Players 2 and 3, after reaching the free-throw-line extended area, break at a sharp angle toward the basket.
6. The player who receives the pass takes the layup shot.
7. The next three players at the baseline recover the ball and begin the drill the other way.

Teaching Points

1. Stress keeping the lanes wide and straight.
2. Insist on good passing techniques.
3. The middle man always stops at or above the free-throw line and moves to the edge of the lane in the direction of his pass. This move places him in a position to receive a return pass.
4. Players should maintain concentration—be ready at all times.
5. Shooting techniques: to develop this drill, have the middle man or the wing players take short jump shots as well as the layup shot.

Drill 13   Three-Line Full
Court Weave Layup Drill

1. As in Drill 12, player 1 is positioned in the middle lane, and players 2 and 3 are in the outside lanes.
2. Player 1 begins the drill by giving a good two-handed lead pass to player 3. Player 1 then cuts behind player 3 to fill the outside lane.
3. Player 3 breaks toward the middle of the court and receives the pass while on the move. Player 3 gives a two-hand chest pass to player 2, and then cuts behind player 2 to fill the left outside lane.
4. Player 2 breaks to the middle toward the area near the top of the free-throw circle, receives the pass from player 3, and looks up court to give a pass to player 1, who should be cutting to the midcourt area. Player 2 follows the pass and goes behind player 1 to fill the right outside lane.
5. Player 1 then gives a pass to player 3 and makes a sharp angle cut toward the top of the free-throw area. Player 1 follows the pass and cuts outside of player 3 to fill the left outside lane.
6. Player 3 dribbles to the free-throw line, makes a two-foot parallel stop, and passes to either player 1 or 2, who after reaching the free-throw-line extended area, makes a sharp cut to the basket. Whichever player receives the ball takes the layup shot. The three players on the baseline continue the drill to the other end of the court after recovering the made shot.

Teaching Points

1. Using good passing techniques.
2. Following up passes by cutting behind the receiver. Players should time this cut so that they will receive the pass while moving toward the basket.
3. Showing hustle in filling the lanes.

FORM SHOOTING DRILLS

Drill 14 Square-Up Shooting Drill

1. There are two lines, one on each side of the foul lane with a coach or manager between the two lines at the edge of the circle near the foul-line extended area. There should be a minimum of six players participating in the drill. The lines will alternate, as one ball is used.
2. Players 1 and 4, or the first two players, make a V-cut to receive the ball, pivot on their inside foot with knees bent, and take the jump shot.
3. The players shoot and follow up their shots. If they miss the jump shot, they rebound and put in a layup shot. After a score, the player passes the ball to the coach or manager and goes to the end of the line at the opposite side.
4. As the ball is returned to the coach, the first player in the opposite line fakes and makes a cut toward the ball and the coach's pass.

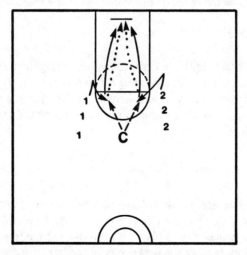

FIGURE 4-4 Square-Up Shooting Drill

Teaching Points

1. Players should make proper movements to receive the ball after faking toward the basket. Emphasize that the player should make the fake as the ball is being passed to the coach and cut to the ball after the coach has received the ball.
2. Players should square off, pivot, and shoot. A player should lift the ball into shooting position as he makes his pivot to square himself to the basket—not after the completion of the pivot.
3. Stress the fundamentals of shooting.
4. Stress shooting from both sides of the court.
5. Players should follow up their shots and learn the rebounding angles.

Drill 15 Square Off to Shoot
After Stopping the Dribble

1. One line is stationed near the sideline at the foul-line extended area on either side of the court. If possible, each player should have a ball.
2. Player 1 dribbles twice toward the baseline, uses a crossover dribble or reverse dribble, and drives to the free-throw line area.
3. The dribbler stops, pivots on the inside foot, and takes a jump shot. He follows up the shot, rebounds, and passes to the next player in line, who continues the drill.
4. The player who rebounds moves to the opposite side of the floor and starts a new line at the foul-line extended area. The drill may continue for a specified period of time; also, the lines may be placed at different positions on the court (for example, on either baseline).

Teaching Points

1. Dribbling techniques that emphasize protecting the ball from the defense.
2. Stopping, pivoting, and squaring off to shoot.
3. Using proper shooting fundamentals after coming to a quick stop.
4. Following up all short jump shots and learning the angles at which a ball will bounce.

Drill 16 Shooting Over a Screen

1. The players are positioned in one line on one side of the court at the foul-line extended area between the foul lane and the sideline. The coach, a manager, or a player is positioned at the front of the line, about five feet away from the first player in the line, to act as the screener.
2. Player 1 has the ball and starts the drill by dribbling toward the screener, stopping, and shooting a jump shot from behind the screen.

3. Player 1 rebounds the shot and dribbles out to the same point on the opposite side of the floor. Player 2 moves across the free-throw line to come behind 1, who sets a screen for player 2.
4. Player 2 shoots, rebounds, and dribbles out to set a screen for player 3 at the opposite side of the floor. Player 1 stays on the left side of the court.
5. This drill can be timed, or the number of baskets made can mark the completion.

Teaching Points

1. Setting up a screen, body balance, and a good handoff should be stressed.
2. Emphasize movement without the ball.
3. Stress the use of the screen to shoot over or to dribble by.

Drill 17 Semicircle Set Shot Drill— Concentrate on Form

1. Players 1 to 10 are positioned in a semicircle about fifteen to eighteen feet from the basket; players 11 and 12 will rebound the shots and feed the shooters. Usually there will be five balls in this drill. (One or two balls may be used with beginning players as the coach checks each player's form.)
2. After a certain period of time, the rebounders will exchange positions with two of the players from the semicircle.

Teaching Point

1. Players should use correct form when shooting the set shot. The coach should check the arc of the shot.

Drill 18 Spot Form Shooting

1. Four lines are positioned with two at the forward positions and two at the corners of the free-throw line. The first player in each line has a ball.
2. Starting with line 1, the first player in each line takes a set shot or jump shot and follows up the shot. After rebounding the shot, player 1 passes to the next player in line and moves to the end of the line.
3. Each player in each line is to take five shots from that position. The lines then rotate clockwise to the next positions.

Teaching Points

1. The shots are to be taken at the eight-to-fifteen-foot range depending on skills of the players.

2. Stress shooting fundamentals and concentration on the target, either the backboard or the rim.
3. The players should follow up their shots and learn to anticipate the angles at which the ball will rebound.

COMPETITIVE DRILLS

Drill 19   Two on a Ball–Spot Shooting Drill (Two Baskets or Six Baskets)

1. The team is divided into pairs with each pair at a basket.
2. The players will practice a particular shot from a certain area on the court. Player 1 shoots ten shots and player 2 rebounds each shot. After ten shots have been taken, the two players change positions.

Teaching Points

1. Correct shooting form.
2. Quick shooting.
3. Quick, accurate passing by the rebounder. The pass should be made to a position where the shooter may handle it easily and go up with a quick shot.

Drill 20   Two Lines–Game Drill

1. This is a competitive shooting drill which may be used at any position; for example, from the corners of the free-throw line and lane.
2. The players in both lines will shoot set shots or jump shots. After shooting, the players will recover the rebound, pass to the next player in line, and then move to the end of the line.
3. The players continue shooting until one line scores ten baskets (or a specified number). The drill may also be timed—for example, thirty seconds or one minute; the line with the most baskets at the end of the elapsed time wins. The lines may exchange positions, or they may be moved to other positions on the court such as the baseline positions.

Teaching Points

1. Stress shooting fundamentals and quickness when shooting. This drill is competitive; the players must shoot against the clock or up to a certain number of shots; however, speed must not replace accuracy.
2. The players can practice shooting from different angles.
3. The players must react quickly to recover the rebound and then get the ball back to the next player.

Drill 21   Jump Shot After Stopping the
Dribble—Square to the Basket, Up Straight

1. The players are positioned in three lines, one at the top of the circle and one at each wing position. The first person in each line has possession of a ball.
2. On a signal from the coach, each player starts a drive to the left. After two dribbles, the players use a crossover (or reverse) dribble and take three quick dribbles to the indicated spots. They stop, pivot, pick up the ball, and take a jump shot.
3. The players go after their own rebounds, pass the ball out to the line they came from, and move to the next line. Player 1 goes to line 2, player 2 goes to line 3, and player 3 goes to line 1.
4. The dribbling moves may vary. That is, players can drive to the left and to different positions.

Teaching Points

1. The players use a quick dribble and make an on-balance stop before attempting the shot.
2. They should pick the ball up quickly as the stop is made and move the ball to the shooting position.
3. The body should be square to the basket as the player prepares to shoot.

Drill 22   Two Lines—Jump Shot,
Bother the Next Shooter

1. Two lines are positioned at each side of the foul lane about five feet from the edge of the foul line.
2. Player 1 takes a jump shot and follows his shot for the rebound or for a recovery of the made shot. After recovering the ball, player 1 passes the ball to player 2 and races, under control and on-balance, to put pressure on player 2, who takes a jump shot. Player 1 then goes to the end of line 2.
3. Player 2 rebounds, passes to the next player in line 1, and moves to put pressure on the shooter. Player 2 goes to the end of line 1.
4. The drill continues for a specific number of shots or for a specific period of time.

Teaching Points

1. Stress correct shooting fundamentals with proper release and follow-through.
2. When shooting under pressure, a player should be ready to receive the pass, move the ball quickly into shooting position, concentrate on the target (the rim or backboard), and not allow the defense to distract him.

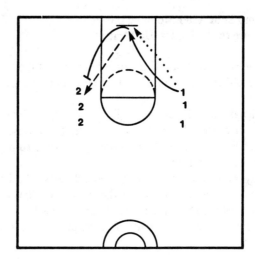

FIGURE 4-5   *Two Lines–Jump Shot, Bother the Next Shooter Drill*

3. Players should follow up all shots taken from these angles and distances. Stress rebounding position and good outlet passes.
4. Emphasize good defensive positioning when approaching the shooter and going up straight when attempting to block a shot and bother the shooter.

Drill 23   Make Two Shots

1. Three lines are positioned at the top of the key and at the two wing positions. The first player in each line has a ball.
2. Each player takes a set shot or a jump shot from the ten-to-fifteen-foot range. The shooter retrieves the ball and goes up for a second, third, or fourth shot until he makes two baskets. After making the second basket, the shooter recovers the ball, dribbles quickly toward the same line, passes to the next player in line, and then moves to the end of the line.
3. The drill continues until one line wins by scoring a predetermined number of shots. The lines will then rotate positions and the drill starts again.

Teaching Points

1. Shooting fundamentals on a variety of shots should be emphasized. Also, the players can learn to shoot in a crowd or with other players very close to them.
2. Emphasize quickness when shooting. The players should be set and in a ready-to-shoot position when waiting for a pass.
3. Stress following the shot, recovering the ball, shooting quickly again, and getting the ball to the next player in line.

4. Competition should be included in this drill, with a penalty for the losers or a prize for the winners.
5. Another aspect of this drill is to require the players to use a fake before shooting after recovering a rebound. A good pump fake and head-and-shoulders fake should be used.

Drill 24   Three Lines–Bother the Shooter

1. Three lines are positioned at midcourt. The player in the middle line has the ball, and lines 2 and 3 are at the wing positions.
2. Player 1 passes to player 3 and goes behind player 3 to fill the outside lane and make a cut toward the basket and the right wing or forward position.
3. Player 3 passes to player 2, who is making a sharp cut toward the free-throw line. Player 3 cuts behind player 2 to fill the outside lane on the left side of the court.
4. Player 2 makes a quick pass to player 1 who is at the corner position. Player 1 is ready to receive the pass and to take a quick jump shot.
5. After passing to player 1, player 2 sprints to put pressure on player 1, who takes the jump shot.
6. Player 3 rebounds and players 1 and 2 break to fill the outlet areas; they are ready to receive the outlet pass from player 3 and start a fast break.
7. Players rotate lines at the completion of the drill. Player 3 goes to line 1, player 1 goes to line 2, and player 2 goes to line 3.

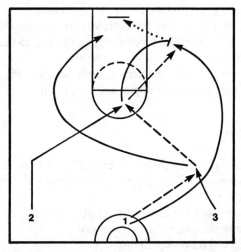

FIGURE 4-6   *Three Lines–Bother the Shooter Drill*

Teaching Points

1. The players should be moving to receive the ball on all passes.
2. The middle man who makes the pass must pass to the shooter in a position that will allow the shooter to shoot quickly.
3. The players can practice jump shooting under pressure by the passer, who will try to block or hinder the shot.

Drill 25 Three Lines—Pass, Cut, and Layup—All Players Shoot

1. Three lines are positioned at midcourt. The first player in the middle line has a ball, and players 2 and 3 start wide at the left and right wing positions near the sidelines.
2. Player 1 starts the drill by passing to player 3, who begins to move toward the basket and toward the center of the court. Player 1 moves behind player 3 and cuts toward the basket.
3. Player 3 passes to player 2, who made his cut toward the top of the key as player 1 made the pass to player 3. After receiving the pass, player 2 stops near the free-throw line and makes a pass to player 1, who drives in for the layup shot.
4. Player 3 continues into the left corner, touches the sideline with his foot, and times his cut to the basket. Player 2 moves to the right corner after passing to player 1.
5. After taking the layup, player 1 retrieves the ball, passes to player 3, and moves to the outlet area on the side to which he passes. Player 3 receives the pass from player 1 and drives in for a layup. He rebounds his shot, passes to player 2, and moves to the outlet area.
6. Player 2 drives for the layup, rebounds, and makes an outlet pass to player 1 or 3. The pass receiver passes the ball to the next player in line 1 at midcourt.
7. The players sprint to midcourt and change lines. Player 1 goes to line 3, player 3 goes to line 2, and player 2 goes to line 1.

Teaching Points

1. Emphasize taking layup shots from different angles and making the correct adjustments and the proper release of the ball when driving along the baseline.
2. All players shoot the layup shots after timing their cut to the ball so that they receive the pass while on the move.
3. Players should follow up all shots.
4. The pass to the cutters should be made softly so that it is easy for the cutter to handle.

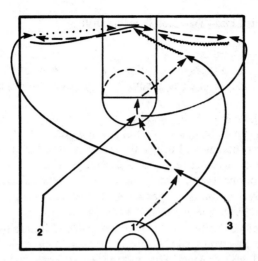

FIGURE 4-7   Three Lines—Pass, Cut, and Layup—All Players Shoot

Drill 26   Four-Spot Shooting with Opposition

1. Four lines are positioned at the two guard and two forward positions. A single player, number 1 in this drill, is positioned under the basket with a ball. Player 1 starts the drill by passing to player 2 and rushes to harass 2, who takes a jump shot. Player 2 follows his shot, rebounds, passes to player 3, and harasses player 3, who takes a jump shot.
2. Player 3 follows the shot, rebounds, passes to player 4, and rushes out to harass player 4. Player 4 takes a jump shot, rebounds, and passes to player 5. Player 4 puts pressure on player 5, who takes a jump shot, rebounds, and passes the ball to the next player in line 1. Player 5 then bothers player 1, who shoots and rebounds. The drill continues for a specified period of time.
3. Each player who makes a pass moves to the end of the line he passes to.

Teaching Points

1. Players practice the shooting fundamentals with special emphasis on lifting the ball and following through.
2. When shooting under pressure, players should concentrate on the target and not allow the defender to distract them.
3. Players should follow their shots and rebound before the ball touches the floor.
4. Players can practice shooting from various positions on the floor.
5. The defensive player should bother the shooter by jumping up straight with his arm fully extended but should not try to block the shot by bringing his arm forward and down.

Drill 27 Four Lines—Two-Ball Shooting Drill

1. Two players are stationed at the baseline near the end of the foul lane. Two lines of players are positioned at the corners of the free-throw line. The first player in lines 1 and 2, at the foul line positions, each has a ball.
2. Player 4 breaks to the foul-lane area to receive a pass from player 1. Player 4 should be in a ready position and moving toward the ball. Player 4 catches the ball and drops his weight to stop his movement. Player 4 then pivots on either foot and takes a jump shot.
3. After shooting, player 4 rebounds or retrieves the ball and passes it to the next player in line 1; player 4 goes to line 2. After passing to player 4, player 1 goes to the end of line 3.
4. Just as player 4 recovers the rebound, player 3 flashes to the foul lane to receive a pass from player 2, pivots, and takes a jump shot. Player 2 moves to line 1 after passing. Player 3 recovers the rebound, passes to line 2, and moves to the end of line 1.

Teaching Points

1. Emphasize moving to receive the ball and being ready to receive the pass while moving. The receiver should have the hands up and give a target to the passer.
2. The pass receiver should set up wide and strong, keeping the ball at about chest level while making a quick pivot.

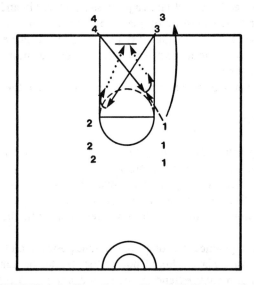

FIGURE 4-8   Four Lines—Two-Ball Shooting Drill

3. A variety of moves may be added to this drill: the shooters may drive for a layup, shoot a hook shot, and also use different fakes to set up their shots.

Drill 28   Five-Spot Shooting

1. Five lines are set up with one line at the top of the key, two lines at each wing position, and two lines in each corner position. The first player in each line has a ball.
2. One line is named to start the movement. For example, player 5 shoots first and rebounds the shot; after rebounding the ball, player 5 passes to the next player in line 5 and goes to the end of the line.
3. As the shot by player 5 hits the rim, player 4 shoots, rebounds, and passes to the next player in the line and goes to the end of line 4. The drill continues with players 3, 2, and 1 following the same procedure.
4. After a certain number of shots, the lines rotate one line to the left and continue the drill.

Teaching Points

1. Emphasize shooting fundamentals with proper balance, release, and follow-through.
2. The shooter should follow the shot and try to recover the rebound before the ball touches the floor.
3. Players should practice shooting from all positions on the floor.
4. Emphasize good passing throughout the drill. Do not allow the players to become careless.

Drill 29   Around-the-World Drill

1. This drill may be used for two or more players. The object of the drill is to score at each position that is marked. The players start at position A and move to B, C, D, and so on; after reaching H, they continue shooting until they return to position A by reversing the order.
2. Player 1 shoots at position A. If player 1 scores, then he or she moves to position B, but, if player 1 misses there will be a second chance. When a player misses a second chance, the player must return to the starting position and begin again.
3. The first player to score from each position is the winner.

Teaching Points

1. Correct shooting techniques.
2. Competition and shooting under pressure.
3. Shooting from different positions on the floor.

4. The drill may be conducted with supervision by the coach, or the players may shoot on their own.

Drill 30 Two-Ball Shooting Drill— Move to Different Positions

1. Players 1 and 2 are positioned at the blocks on either side of the lane and each has a ball. Player 3 is positioned at the free-throw line.
2. Player 1 passes to player 3, who takes a jump shot. Player 1 rebounds the shot and prepares to pass again to player 3. After shooting, player 3 moves to the right and across the foul line ready to receive a pass from player 2.
3. Player 2 gives a quick lead pass to player 3, who pivots on the inside foot and takes a jump shot. Player 2 follows for the rebound and prepares to pass again to player 3. After taking the shot, player 3 moves left across the lane ready for the pass from player 1.
4. Players 1 and 2 continue to pass alternately to player 3 for thirty seconds; then the players rotate positions. As many baskets as are available may be used by the total squad.

Teaching Points

1. Stress proper footwork when moving into position for a shot and getting ready to receive the pass.
2. The shooter should release the ball quickly but should not rush the shot. Emphasize that speed should not replace accuracy.

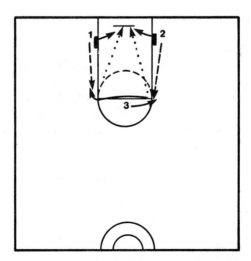

FIGURE 4-9 Two-Ball Shooting—Move to Different Positions

3. The shooter's hands should be in a ready position at all times so that he or she may receive and lift the ball into shooting position without wasting time or effort.

Drill 31   Foul Shooting—Two Teams Oppose Each Other and Must Make a Certain Number of Shots in Succession

1. The two groups are given a specific number of free throws in succession (e.g., six, seven, eight).
2. Each player takes one shot and moves to the next position to the left. The players who are waiting along the sides of the lanes will practice the correct rebounding technique from the position in which they are located.
3. The coach moves from group to group and checks on the correct rebounding techniques as well as proper shooting techniques.

Teaching Point

1. Concentrate on having players make the free throw under pressure. The shots must be made consecutively so that each player experiences the pressure of making important shots.

Drill 32   Two Baskets—Shoot One and One—Make the First

1. The players are positioned at two or more baskets with three, four, five or six players at each basket.
2. Each player shoots the free throws from a one-on-one situation. If the first shot is made, then the player shoots a second shot. If the first shot is missed, the shooter steps off the line, moves to the baseline near the sideline, and runs a quick sprint the length of the floor and back.
3. The next player takes a shot using the same procedure. The players run only after a miss of the first shot.

Teaching Point

1. The shooter has to concentrate on the first free throw and to make it, so that shooter and that team will have an opportunity to take a second shot.

Drill 33   Six Baskets—Rotation to Next Basket After a Made Shot

1. The team is divided into equal groups at each of six baskets (or as many as are available).
2. Each player takes one shot and then moves to the next basket on his left.

Player 1 is the shooter and player 2 is the rebounder, who works on timing when stepping into the lane as well as on the rebounding technique.

3. After player 1 shoots, he or she moves to the position 2 at the next basket
   on his left. Player 2 rebounds, and then moves to the foul lane into player
   1's position, and shoots a free throw.
4. The players rotate so that the situation will be more game-like: every
   free throw situation is different in a game—a person does not get to shoot
   five, ten, or more shots in succession.

Teaching Points

1. The players should be reminded that they should be mentally ready when
   they step to the line and receive the ball from the official. They should
   know exactly how they will stand during the preliminaries and during the
   actual shot.
2. Stepping to the free throw line in this manner is much more realistic, and
   practicing in this manner is much more beneficial.

Drill 34   Free-Throw Rebounding

1. Two teams of five players each are used. The 0 team is the offensive or
   shooting team with player 4 ready to shoot a free throw. The X team is
   the defensive team.
2. Player 4 is placed in a one-on-one situation. If player 4 makes both free
   throws, the shooting team rotates clockwise: player 1 to position 2, 2
   to 3, 3 to 5, 5 to 4, and 4 to 1. If a player misses a free throw, the teams
   rebound as in a game situation. If the shooting team rebounds, they return the ball for the free throw to their next shooter and the drill continues.
3. If the defense rebounds, they become the shooting team, and both teams
   rotate clockwise.
4. The first team to reach twenty points is the winner (or a number determined by the coach).

Teaching Points

1. Fundamentals of free-throw shooting.
2. Shooting in a game-like situation.
3. Rebounding in a game-like situation.
4. This is a good drill with which to finish practice. The losers take sprints.

5

Individual Offensive Moves

INTRODUCTION

Successful team offenses must be built upon good individual offensive fundamentals. These fundamentals include shooting, passing, rebounding, dribbling, cutting, and setting picks. The combination of the individual movements contributes to the development of the team offense. In other words, a team can better execute its offensive system when the players have developed their individual offensive skills.

This chapter deals with individual offensive moves. Coaches may begin with drills involving the implementation of basic techniques. Then the drills are practiced in various individual positions, such as the point guard position, wing position, the pivot area, and so on. The next step in the progression of competitive drills is the use of two-on-two, three-on-three, and finally team drills to improve individual skills to benefit the team's offensive system.

With this thought in mind, a coach who has prepared an offensive system will work to help his players master the individual skills that are necessary to the success of his offense. There is no substitute for proper execution. The patterns, whether simple or complicated, will not be effective unless the players can execute the fundamentals.

TRIPLE-THREAT FOOTWORK

Drill 1   Individual Offensive Moves—
With the Ball—Use Six Baskets

A. Fake Shot and Drive

1. Player 1 uses his left foot as the pivot foot and drives by stepping with the right foot.
2. The offensive player uses head and shoulder fakes and holds the ball at a position between the belt and the chest.
3. The ball handler fakes a shot to bring the defensive player up and out of the defensive stance.
4. When the defensive player is off balance, the driver steps off with his right foot, pushes the ball out in front, and goes in for the layup. The offensive player retrieves the ball, passes to the next player in line, and moves to basket B on his left.

B. Fake Drive and Shoot

1. Player 2 takes a jab step to get the defensive player to back off.
2. Player 2 takes a step back and takes a shot over the left shoulder of the defensive man. Player 2 retrieves the ball, passes it back to the next player, and goes to basket C to the left.

C. Double Fake

1. Player 4 fakes a drive by taking a jab step and then settles back on his heels.
2. As player 4 brings his weight back, he fakes a shot by bringing his head and shoulders up.
3. Player 4 then takes a jab step, pushes the ball out in front, takes two dribbles, stops, and goes up for the jump shot.
4. Player 4 follows up the shot, passes the ball back to the next player, and goes left to basket D.

D. Rocker Step

1. Player 5 fakes a drive, making a jab step over the front foot of the defense.
2. He brings his foot back to the starting position.
3. His weight rests on his heels; he should not bring his feet back, only his head and shoulders.
4. When the defensive player comes back, player 5 takes a left-front-foot

drive to the hoop. He retrieves the ball, passes to the next player, and goes to basket E.

E. Basket

1. Player 6 takes a jab step toward the basket and steps back with both feet parallel.
2. He pivots on both feet and steps across the defense with the same foot used to fake.
3. He pushes the ball out in front of him and drives to the basket.
4. He retrieves the ball, passes to the next player, and goes to the left to basket F.

F. Basket–Jump Shot Off the Step

1. The left foot is the pivot foot. The defense is close enough to stop the set shot and far enough away to prevent the drive.
2. He takes the jab step and, as the defense reacts, goes straight up with the jump shot. He retrieves the ball, passes to the next player, and goes to basket A.

Teaching Points

1. Stress fundamentals.
2. Quickness.
3. Saving the dribble, as a means to get straight to the basket.

FAKE-AND-DRIVE DRILLS

Drill 2 One-on-One from the Wing Position

1. The coach is positioned at the top of the key with the basketball.
2. Offensive player 1 and defensive player X1 are positioned at the foul-line extended area about five feet from the sideline. Other teammates are positioned in two lines along the baseline and outside the sideline.
3. Player X1 starts in a denial defensive position in order to force offensive player 1 to move and fake to get free for a pass from the coach.
4. The coach passes the ball to player 1, who will turn to face the basket and try to drive toward it or maneuver to a position that will provide a relatively easy shot. Player X1 tries to prevent easy movement or an easy score by player 1. The drill continues until player 1 scores or player X1 recovers the rebound.
5. The ball is returned to the coach by the defensive player. Player X1 goes to line 1 and player 1 goes to line X1.

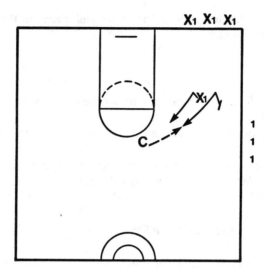

FIGURE 5-1   One-on-One from the Wing Position

Teaching Points

1. The offensive player must make an attempt to score before "four count" is reached (a-thousand-one, a-thousand-two, a-thousand-three, and so on).
2. The offensive player may return the ball to the coach and move again to get free to a position to make another offensive play.
3. If the defensive player forces the offensive player to turn his back while dribbling, the player should be stopped and the defensive player given credit for a "stop."
4. A strong denial position by player X1 at the start of the drill.

Drill 3   One-on-One from the Corner

1. The same procedure as in Drill 2 with the lines and the coach in the positions designated.

CUTS TO RECEIVE THE BALL

**Drill 4   One-on-One from the Top of
the Key—Roll the Ball to the Offense**

1. The offensive players are positioned at a point between the midcourt line and the top of the key.
2. The defensive players are positioned along the baseline.

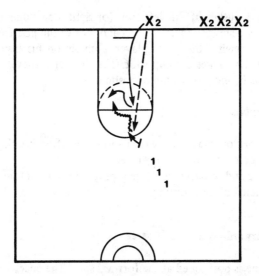

FIGURE 5-2   *One-on-One from the Top of the Key—Roll the Ball to the Offense*

3. Player X2 rolls the ball in the direction of the top of the key toward player 1, who moves quickly to gain possession of the ball.
4. After rolling the ball, player X1 sprints quickly to a defensive position near the top of the key and tries to prevent player 1's offensive movement toward the basket. Player X1 goes to line 1 and 1 goes to line X1.

Teaching Points

1. The offensive player is restricted to making a drive within the limits of the foul-line extended area. If the player dribbles outside of this lane or turns his back, the defensive player is given credit for the "stop."
2. The defensive player should approach the offensive player 1 quickly, on-balance, and ready to force the offensive player to move in only one direction—then be ready to react in that direction and take it away. "Show an opening and then take it away."
3. The defensive players may be directed to overplay the offensive player's strong hand and force him to use his weak hand when dribbling.

Drill 5   V-Cut High, Square
Off for a Jump Shot

1. The players are positioned in a single line at the free-throw-line extended area. The first player in the line plays defense. The coach has possession of the ball at the top of the key.
2. The offensive player fakes a cut toward the basket and then breaks toward the foul line, ready to receive a pass from the coach.

3. Player 1 pushes off his left foot (or right, depending on the side of the floor) and steps to meet the ball and receive the pass from the coach.
4. After receiving the pass, player 1 pivots on his inside foot, faces the basket, and takes a jump shot. The shooter retrieves the ball, passes to the coach, and goes to the opposite line.

Teaching Points

1. Footwork on the V-cut, which allows the offensive player to cut in front of the defense in order to get free.
2. Pivoting and squaring off to gain proper balance before taking the shot.
3. Fundamentals of shooting.

Drill 6   Forward—Weak-Side Cutter

1. One line is positioned at the forward spot. The coach has the ball outside the foul lane on the opposite side of the court.
2. Player 3 moves forward, takes a jab step with the left foot toward the baseline, steps with the opposite foot, and then cuts toward the basket (or the player jab-steps with the right foot and moves in the opposite direction toward the basket).
3. When the offensive player cuts across the foul lane, the hands should be ready to receive the ball. Upon receiving the ball, the player takes a layup, rebounds, gives the ball to the coach, and goes to the opposite side of the floor to start a line at the forward position.

Teaching Point

1. Emphasize footwork by the cutter, who must make a good fake and a strong, hard cut to the ball. Stress taking a hard step, pushing off the faking foot, and moving to the ball with hands ready.

Drill 7   V-Cut, Layup Drill

1. There are two lines at the wing positions on each side of the free-throw lane. The coach is at the top of the free-throw area with the ball.
2. The first player in line 2 makes a step toward the coach, then makes a reverse cut to the basket. He receives the pass and goes in for a layup shot. Player 2 rebounds the shot and passes the ball to the coach.
3. As the pass is made to the coach from player 2, the first player in line 1 makes a step toward the coach and makes a reverse cut to the basket, looking for the pass from the coach.
4. The drill continues as each player retrieves the ball, passes to the coach, and goes to the end of the opposite line.

Teaching Points

1. Footwork—the players should go straight toward the ball and push off hard away from the ball.
2. Receiving the ball—as a player cuts, the hands should be up and ready to receive the ball.

Drill 8 V-Cut from the Forward
Position for a Layup or a Jump Shot

1. The line is positioned in the corner at the forward position. The coach, with the ball, is at the guard position.
2. Player 3 makes a move toward the baseline, pushes off the foot closest to the baseline, and steps to receive the pass from the coach.
3. The player can drive to the basket for the layup or can square up and take a jump shot.
4. The player retrieves the ball, passes back to the coach, and goes to the opposite forward position to begin a new line. When the ball is returned to the coach, the next player in line makes a fake and moves to the ball. The drill continues until each player has taken a turn.

Teaching Points

1. Stress pushing off one foot, staying low, and moving toward the ball.
2. When receiving the ball, the hands should be kept ready to receive the ball, using the block-and-tuck technique.

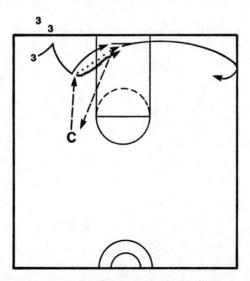

FIGURE 5-3 *V-Cut from the Forward Position for a Layup or a Jump Shot*

3. Stress putting the ball out in front on a long, low, hard drive.
4. Players should follow up their shots and be reminded always to go after rebounds.

Drill 9 Give and Go—Pass and Cut

1. The players are positioned in two lines at the forward and guard positions.
2. Player 2 passes to player 4, fakes a cut toward the foul line, and then breaks to the basket looking for a return pass from player 4.
3. Player 4 gives a return pass to player 2 and follows the pass to the basket, ready to rebound a missed shot.
4. The players exchange lines after completion of their part of the drill.

Teaching Points

1. Correct timing on the cut to the basket.
2. Making the passes in such a manner that the receiver will be able to handle them easily and be in a position to make an effective move after receiving the ball.

Drill 10 Give and Go—Pass and Go Behind for a Handoff

1. The players are positioned in two lines at the forward and guard positions.

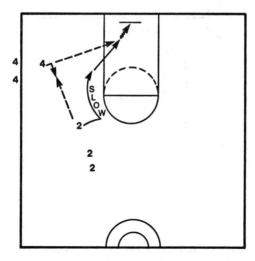

FIGURE 5-4   Give and Go—Pass and Cut

2. Player 2 passes to player 4, fakes a cut to the basket, and moves behind player 4 to receive a handoff from him.
3. Player 4, upon receiving the pass, stays in a triple-threat position in order to protect the ball and be ready to drive, shoot, or pass.
4. After receiving the handoff from player 4, player 2 drives to the basket. Player 4 makes a reverse pivot, rolls to the basket after making the handoff, and looks for a return pass or goes for the rebound.

Teaching Points

1. Movement to receive the ball—it is the responsibility of the player receiving the ball to use the pick or screen correctly.
2. Passing techniques—always practice as if in game conditions. Players should make every pass a perfect pass.
3. Correct footwork on pivots—player 2 steps toward the foul line, steps off his right foot and moves toward player 4. After giving the ball back to player 2, player 4 pivots on the foot closest to the foul lane and rolls toward the basket with hands ready.

Drill 11 Push Pass to a Forward

1. Two lines are positioned at the guard and wing areas on either side of the court. The first player in the line of guards has a ball.
2. As player 1 begins to dribble toward player 3, player 3 starts to move toward the dribbler but stops quickly and changes direction by pushing off his front foot. Player 3 cuts toward the basket, ready to receive a pass from player 1.
3. Player 1 stops the dribble and makes a push pass, either a bounce or chest pass, to player 3, who is cutting to the basket.
4. Players exchange lines and also move to the opposite side of the floor, at the completion of the series on one side.

Teaching Points

1. Using correct technique for changing direction and cutting to the basket.
2. Keeping the hands ready to receive the ball at all times.
3. Making the push pass very quickly after stopping and picking up the dribble.

**Drill 12 Inside Handoff or Drop
Pass to the Guard—Give and Go**

1. The players are positioned in two lines at the guard and wing positions on either side of the court.
2. Player 1 passes to player 3, who fakes and moves to receive the ball.

3. After the pass, player 1 makes a fake as if to cut behind player 3 but cuts in front of him, ready to receive a pass.
4. As player 1 goes by, player 3 makes a drop pass or a handoff to player 1, who turns and drives to the basket for a layup. Player 3 follows the pass and cuts to the basket for the rebound.

Teaching Points

1. Stress correct footwork when making the cut toward the basket.
2. Emphasize a quick but gentle or light touch on the release when making the drop pass or the handoff.

Drill 13 Give and Go

1. Players are positioned in two lines at the guard positions.
2. Player 1 passes to player 2 and either takes steps away from the direction of the pass and cuts to the basket or moves toward the ball and then cuts to the basket. As player 1 cuts to the basket, the hands are held ready to receive a pass from player 2.
3. Player 2 steps to meet the ball and receives the pass from player 1. Player 2 returns the pass to player 1 on a give-and-go play and follows for the rebound.

Teaching Points

1. Emphasize that players should step to meet all passes.
2. Stress correct footwork when faking, cutting, and moving to receive the ball.
3. Players should follow up shots and rebound every shot.

Drill 14 Pass and Go Behind

1. Two lines are positioned at the guard positions.
2. Player 2 steps to meet the pass from player 1. As player 2 receives the ball from player 1, player 2 stays in a crouched position, protects the ball, and pivots to a position from which he may shoot, pass, or drive.
3. Player 1 fakes toward the basket and goes behind player 2 to receive a return handoff. Players 1 and 2 can run a pick and roll play, or player 1 may drive or shoot from behind player 2's screen.

Teaching Points

1. Movement to receive a pass.
2. The fundamentals of a pick and roll play must be emphasized—the cutter

must fake and run the defensive player into the screen so that he will force the defense to switch or become confused.

PIVOT MOVES TO RECEIVE THE BALL

Drill 15   Low Pivot—Flash to the Ball

1. Player 5 is stationed in the low-pivot position and the coach is in the forward position with the ball.
2. Player 5 fakes one way with a jab step and cuts the other way toward the ball.
3. As player 5 moves into the lane, the hands are ready to receive the ball. When player 5 receives the ball in the lane, he may take a hook shot, make a power layup move, or make a reverse move for either a hook shot, layup, or jump shot.

Teaching Points

1. Good footwork—the player should work to get good position with his body between the ball and the defensive player.
2. Good body balance on cuts—the player should move toward the coach in a balanced position with one hand giving a signal for the ball.

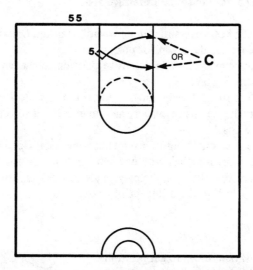

FIGURE 5-5   Low Pivot—Flash to the Ball

3. Individual offensive moves—as the players' skills develop, the coach will stress a greater variety of moves.

Drill 16   Low-Pivot Flash to the High Pivot

1. The players are positioned in a line behind the baseline and to the side of the lane. The first player in the line is positioned at the side of the lane near the block.
2. On a signal from the coach, player 5 makes a jab step into the lane and then cuts toward the foul line ready to receive a pass from the coach.
3. After receiving the pass, player 5 turns to face the basket and is ready to pass, shoot, or drive. In this drill player 5 fakes a shot and drives to the basket.
4. Player 5 rebounds the shot and gives the ball to the next player in line and moves to the end of the line. The next player passes the ball to the coach, fakes, and cuts to the foul line ready for the pass from the coach. The drill continues for as many repetitions as desired by the coach. (The players may alternate cutting from both sides.)

Teaching Points

1. The player who receives the pass should keep the ball up and in a position where it cannot be knocked away.
2. Emphasize various fakes by the pivot man to get free to receive the pass from the coach.

Drill 17   Big Man—Go to the Defensive Man

1. The coach has a ball and is in a forward position. One offensive player, 5, is in the weak-side, low-pivot position.
2. Defensive player X5 is in defensive position in the lane between the ball and offensive player 5.
3. Player 5 must get free by moving across the lane, positioning himself very close to the defensive player, and then cutting to the ball for the pass from the coach.
4. Player 5 uses one hand as a target for the pass. Upon receiving the pass, player 5 blocks the ball with one hand and clamps it with the other.
5. After receiving the pass, the players are to work on offensive moves, such as the hook shot, the dribble, and power layup.

Teaching Points

1. Players should move to get position.
2. The offensive player should adjust his or her position as the defense moves,

remaining close to the defensive player so that he or she may cut quickly to the ball and receive the pass. Emphasize that the offensive player should stay close to the defensive player so that he or she may know where he or she is at all times and will be able to control the defender.

Drill 18   Big Man—Overplay One Side

1. The coach is on the wing position with a ball. Offensive player 5 is in the strong-side, low-pivot position. Defensive player X5 overplays on either side.
2. Offensive player 5 should place the elbow against the defensive player's hip, take a wide stance, and try to seal or pin the defensive player behind him or on his side.
3. Player 5 should use the hand away from the defense as a target for the pass from the coach.
4. Offensive player 5, upon receiving the ball, should work on moves to the basket.

Teaching Points

1. Stress the fundamentals of getting position and emphasize that the foot closer to the defense should be slightly forward so that the defender cannot move to a fronting position.
2. Players should have good body position in receiving the ball.

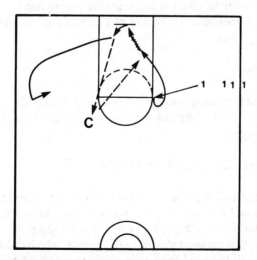

FIGURE 5-6   Reverse Cut from the Forward Position

Drill 19 Reverse Cut from the Forward Position

1. The players are stationed in one line at the forward position and the coach is at the corner of the foul line with the ball.
2. Player 1 makes a move toward the coach as if to receive a pass at the foul line. Using either a parallel or stride stop, player 1 reverses and breaks toward the basket with his hands ready to receive a pass.
3. The coach makes a pass to the player who drives in for a layup. The player rebounds the shot, passes back to the coach, and goes to the opposite side of the court. The drill continues with the second player in the line starting a move as the ball is passed to the coach.

Teaching Point

1. Movement without the ball—players should make a straight hard cut to the ball with hands ready to receive it and make a reverse pivot by pushing off their inside foot. As a player reverses, he or she stays low with hands out in front, ready to receive the pass.

Drill 20 Back-Door or Reverse Cut

1. The players are placed in three positions—guard, wing, and low pivot.
2. Player 1 passes to player 5, who flashes to the high-pivot position at the foul line, and moves away from the ball, either to the left or right.
3. Player 3 takes steps toward the middle, then, pushing off the inside foot, makes a reverse cut to the basket. Player 5 gives a bounce pass to player 3 for a layup; player 5 then rolls away from the ball and toward the basket, ready to rebound and make the pass to line 1.
4. Player 5 goes back to the end of line 5 at the baseline. Players 1 and 3 exchange lines.

Teaching Point

1. Emphasize moving without the ball and timing the cut to the basket. Player 3 should fake and time the cut just as player 5 receives the pass from player 1.

Drill 21 Pivot Player Gets Free for a Pass

1. Pivot player 5 starts at the middle of the free-throw line. Players 1, 2, 3, 4, 6, and 7 (or more players) are positioned in guard, wing, and corner positions. Player X5 plays in a denial position against player 5 and starts in a position between player 5 and player 1, who has the ball.
2. As the ball is passed from player to player (1 to 3 to 1 to 2 to 4 to 6), pivot player 5 moves to get free. Player 5 may use fakes, turns, pivots,

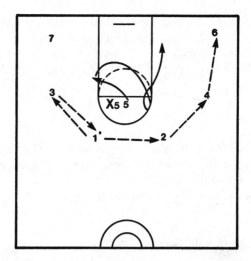

FIGURE 5-7 *Pivot Player Gets Free for a Pass*

changes of direction, and other moves to get free to receive a pass from a player on the perimeter.

3. If player 5 receives the pass, he may use his offensive scoring moves against player X5 or return the ball to one of the offensive players and then move to a better position to receive another pass.

Teaching Points

1. Players should pass quickly so that the pass is made when the pivot is moving to the open position.
2. The pivot man makes various moves. The hands should be ready for a pass at any time.
3. The pivot player should set up wide and occupy as much space as possible so that he can keep player X5 on his back or to his side. This will enable him to present a good target to the passer and to receive the ball in a position that will allow him to make a quick move to the basket.

SCREENING DRILLS

Drill 22   Pass and Screen

1. Two lines are positioned at the guard positions.
2. Player 1 passes to player 2, who steps to meet the pass. After player 1 passes, he or she fakes a cut to the basket and moves to set a pick for player 2. The pick is to be set three feet from the defensive player.

3. Player 2 uses a jab step one way and dribbles off the pick the opposite way, or takes a shot from behind the screen.
4. After player 2 moves off the screen or shoots, player 1 reverse-pivots, cuts toward the basket, and follows the shot by player 2. Players exchange lines.

Teaching Points

1. Stress how to set the pick or screen. In this drill, player 1 sets a pick to the side and about three feet from player 2. Player 1 must not move but wait for player 2 to drive.
2. Defensive players may be added to the drill.

Drill 23   Pick and Roll—Give and Go

1. Two lines are stationed at the guard positions. Player 2 has the ball and starts the drill by passing to player 1.
2. After passing, player 2 fakes a cut to the basket and moves to set a pick for player 1.
3. As player 1 drives off the pick, player 2 pivots to face the ball and then cuts to the basket.
4. Player 1 makes a pass to player 2, who then drives for a layup shot.
5. Both players go for the rebound, return the ball to the next player in line, and then move to the end of the opposite line.

Teaching Points

1. The pass receivers should step to meet the ball while giving a target.
2. Stress how to set the pick. The player setting the screen goes to a spot to pick off the defensive player. The screener faces toward the outside of the court.
3. Footwork going off the pick is important. The player with the ball may jab-step left or right, dribble the opposite way, and move very close to the player setting the pick. Player 1 can use the crossover or reverse dribble.
4. Watch for good footwork on the reverse pivot by the player who sets the pick. As player 1 dribbles off the pick to the right, the screener pivots on the foot closest to the baseline, staying low and on balance to screen off the defensive player, and then rolls or steps toward the basket. The hands should be ready to receive the ball.

Drill 24   Dribble Screen and Handoff

1. Two lines are stationed at the guard positions. Player 1 has the ball and begins the drill by dribbling toward the defensive player guarding player 2.

2. Player 2 fakes one way and moves toward player 1. The hands should be ready to receive the ball.
3. As player 1 approaches player 2, he or she sets a pick and hands off the ball on the outside shoulder.
4. Player 2 receives a handoff pass from player 1 and drives to the basket. After making the handoff, player 1 pivots and rolls to the basket, either to make a return pass or to rebound.
5. The players exchange lines.

Teaching Points

1. Emphasize the fundamentals of a pick.
2. Stress the techniques of dribbling when being closely guarded. The player should keep his body between the ball and the defense.
3. Players should move correctly without the ball in order to set up the screen. Player 2 must jab-step to the right and then move to the left. Player 2 then cuts as close to the pick as possible in order to run the imaginary defensive player into the pick.

Drill 25   Fake-the-Dribble Screen and Keep the Ball

1. There are two lines at the guard positions. Player 2 has the ball and starts the drill by dribbling to the left.
2. Player 2 dribbles toward player 1, who fakes to the left and cuts toward player 2 as if to receive the handoff.
3. As player 2 approaches player 1, it appears a pick will be set. Instead of waiting for the pick, player 2 uses a change-of-pace dribble and drives by player 1 to the basket. Player 1 follows for the rebound.
4. The players change lines.

Teaching Points

1. Emphasize dribbling techniques. Player 2 should use a slow speed on the dribble toward player 1. As player 1 comes in to set a pick, player 2 increases speed and moves off in back of player 1.
2. Stress timing. This can be accomplished only through practice.

Drill 26   Inside Screen by the Dribbler with a Pick-and-Roll Play—Guard and Forward

1. The players are positioned at the guard and forward areas.

2. Player 1 dribbles toward player 3, who jab-steps toward the baseline and comes around player 1 looking to receive a handoff pass.
3. Player 1 picks up the ball and positions the feet in such a manner as to allow him to pivot and set a screen as he hands off.
4. As player 3 receives the ball, he drives toward the basket for the layup. Player 1 rolls to the basket after making the handoff.

Teaching Points

1. Fundamentals of dribbling—player 1 should dribble toward the lane, then use a crossover dribble and move to set the pick for his teammate.
2. Using the pick—the forward (player 3) must step toward the baseline to make the defensive player move the opposite way. Player 3 then cuts off the back of the pick to receive the ball.

Drill 27   Dribble—Outside Screen with Pick and Roll

1. Players are positioned at guard and forward; player 1 has the ball.
2. As player 1 dribbles toward the corner of the foul line, player 3 steps toward the baseline and then moves to set the pick for player 1.
3. Player 1 dribbles off the pick, and player 3 reverses to face the ball and rolls to the basket. Player 1 can jump shoot, drive for a layup, or pass to player 3.

Teaching Points

1. Stress the pick.
2. Also stress the importance of the player with the ball using the pick.

Drill 28   Two-Man Play

1. The players are positioned in four lines, two at each of the guard and forward positions. The guards are numbered 1 and 2; the forwards are called 3 and 4.
2. Player 2 passes to player 4 and moves to set a pick for him. Forwards 2 and 4 use a pick-and-roll play.
3. As players 2 and 4 are making a pick-and-roll move, players 1 and 3 move to exchange places with each other in order to keep the defense busy.
4. If the first two players are unsuccessful, player 4 passes crosscourt to player 1 or 3, who will make the two-man play on the other side of the court.

Teaching Points

1. Stress the fundamentals of the pick and roll.

2. Emphasize proper movement without the ball by players on the weak side in order to keep their defensive men occupied as well as to free themselves for a pass.
3. Starting with these two-on-two drills and moving up to five-player drills, the coach should look for and constantly stress the ideas of moving without the ball at all times.

MULTIPLAYER DRILLS

Drill 29   Three-Man Play and Screen Away

1. The players are positioned in three lines. One line is at the top of the key while the other two are at the wings. Player 1 has the ball.
2. Player 1 passes the ball on the right side to player 2, who makes a fake and moves to receive the ball from player 1.
3. Player 1 moves to the opposite side to set a pick for player 3 at the foul-line extended area. Player 3 fakes toward the baseline, cuts off the pick by player 1, and moves to the basket looking to receive a pass from player 2.
4. Player 1 rolls back toward the ball after player 3 cuts off the pick. Player 2 may pass to player 3 for a layup or to player 1 for a jump shot. The players rotate lines after the completion of each series.
5. Player 1 moves to line 2, player 2 moves to line 3, and player 3 moves to line 1.

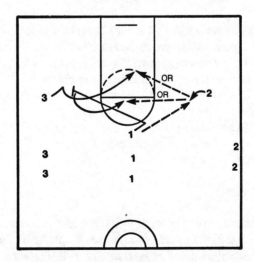

FIGURE 5-8   Three-Man Play and Screen Away

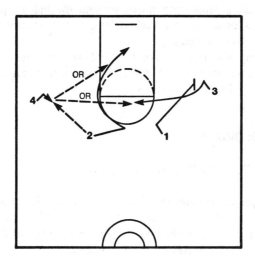

FIGURE 5-9 Four-Man Play from Four Lines

Teaching Points

1. Emphasize making the passes quickly and to the hand away from the defensive player.
2. Stress the fundamentals of picks and rolls.
3. Most often, the player who sets the screen will be free to receive the pass if he learns to set it correctly.

Drill 30 Four-Man Play from Four Lines

1. The players are positioned in four lines at the guard and forward positions.
2. Player 2 passes to player 4, fakes as if to follow the pass, and cuts to the basket on a give-and-go play. Player 2 continues to the corner on the ball side if he does not receive the pass from player 4.
3. Player 1 screens for player 3, who cuts across the foul line toward the ball.
4. Player 4 can pass to player 2 or 3.
5. The players exchange positions so that they will be able to practice on both sides of the court.

Teaching Points

1. Emphasize the fundamentals of the give and go—as player 2 cuts through, his hands should be ready and his eyes should be on the ball at all times.
2. Emphasize movement away from the ball. Players 1 and 3 are always moving; as the ball comes back to the right side, players 2 and 4 will move to the ball so that there is continuous movement.

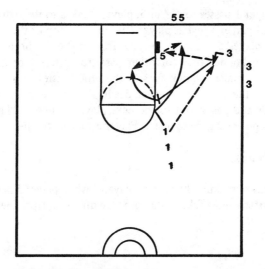

FIGURE 5-10 *Scissors Cut Off the Low Pivot*

Drill 31   Scissors Cut Off the Low Pivot

1. The players are positioned in three lines. Player 1 is at the guard position, player 3 is at the forward position, and player 5 is in the low-pivot position.
2. Player 1 passes to player 3 and moves toward the foul lane, as if making a cut to the basket.
3. Player 3 passes to player 5, who has established his position near the block, and player 3 moves toward the foul lane to screen for player 1, who cuts toward the ball and is ready to receive a pass from player 5.
4. Player 5 can pass to player 1 for a jump shot (A) or to player 3, who moves to the basket after setting the screen for player 1 (B).

Teaching Points

1. Stress movement without the ball.
2. Stress passing to the pivot man as well as by the pivot man.

Drill 32   Split the Post—Pass and
Cut—Receive a Return Pass

1. The players are positioned in two lines at the guard positions and in one line at the baseline. They are numbered 1 and 2 at the guard positions and 5 in the pivot position.
2. Player 5 breaks from the baseline to the foul line and receives a pass from player 1. Player 1 passes to player 5, fakes left, and cuts to the right and toward the basket ready to receive a pass from player 5.

3. As player 1 passes to player 5, player 2 fakes to the right and cuts off the back of player 1 just as player 1 reaches the top of the key.

4. After player 5 receives the pass from player 1, he pivots and looks to throw a bounce pass (or other pass) to cutters 1 or 2. The cutter may shoot or make a quick pass to the other cutter. For example, player 2 receives the pass from player 5 and shoots the layup shot. Player 1 rebounds and passes out to the next player in line 1. Player 1 goes to line 2, and player 2 goes to line 1. Player 5 returns to lines.

Teaching Points

1. Emphasize making the pass to player 5 while player 5 is moving.
2. The cutters must fake in the opposite direction from the cut.

6

Rebounding Drills

INTRODUCTION

With the exception of shooting, rebounding is considered by many coaches the most important fundamental in the game of basketball, since "you must have the ball in order to score." The important elements in rebounding are position, body balance, timing, jumping, and protecting the ball.

Individual rebounding technique simply means getting the body into a well-balanced position, timing the jump, retrieving the ball by grasping it firmly, and then landing in a good position in order to get the ball to a teammate or attempt to score immediately.

The early drills in this chapter are concerned with individual drills which emphasize technique. The drills progress into two-man, three-man, four-man, and so on, and then team rebounding. A second aspect of the drills is the emphasis placed upon the idea of competition. The drills should not end until a basket is scored or the defensive player gains possession of the ball. These drills must be repeated throughout the season since there must be a continual strengthening of the fundamentals.

FUNDAMENTAL DRILL WITHOUT A BALL

Drill 1 Defensive Technique—No Ball

1. The players pair up and establish one-on-one positions over the full length of the court. The purpose of this drill is to help the defensive player develop the skills and techniques of boxing out.

2. The coach can give a signal such as "to the right." On this signal, all offensive players will take two steps to their right.
3. As the offensive player moves, the defensive player pivots on the left foot, swings the body around and moves into the box-out position. The player should be in a semicrouch position with the posterior extended into the offensive player's thighs.
4. Players' arms should be bent and extended to each side so that the offensive player cannot go around them, while their hands should be ready to retrieve the ball.
5. The eyes of the defensive player should be on the waist and hips of the offensive player so that he may better know the way the offensive player will move. As the defensive player boxes out, his eyes turn to the basket to find the basketball.

Teaching Points

1. Defensive stance—emphasize using the eyes and what part of the play to watch.
2. Correct footwork and positioning—these will allow the defensive player to make contact before the offensive player can begin his move.
3. Aggressiveness in maintaining the box-out position—remind players that their arms may be up and out but they cannot intentionally hook their opponent.
4. Looking for the basketball—this should be constantly emphasized.

FUNDAMENTAL DRILLS WITH A BALL

Drill 2 Offensive and Defensive
Techniques—Six Baskets

1. If possible, this may be a six-station drill emphasizing rebounding from all the different angles on the court. At all the stations, the defensive player may use either the step-in or pivot method to box out. It is advisable to practice both methods.
2. In location A, the offensive player can go left or right from the free-throw line.
3. At location B, the defensive player boxes out after the offensive player has taken the shot. The defensive rebounder should try to force the offense one way or the other.
4. At location C, the defensive player is boxing out after a shot has been taken by the coach or manager from the strong side or the opposite side of the floor. Since the high percentage of the rebounds will bounce at an angle toward the baseline on the opposite side, the defensive player should establish a position that forces the offensive player toward the middle of the court.

5. At location D, the offensive player is positioned with his back to the basket in the high-pivot position at the foul line. The defensive player must work on good position and box out as the offensive player moves to rebound the shot taken by the coach.
6. At location E, use the same moves as at location B but on the opposite side of the floor. Here, emphasis should be put on strong-side and weak-side rebounding.
7. At location F, the offensive player plays low pivot. The coach must stress that the defensive player establishes immediate position and contact.

Teaching Points

1. Good body balance and footwork.
2. Techniques of rebounding.
3. Use of these techniques from different positions on the floor.

Drill 3   Mikan Drill Variation

1. One or two players are positioned at each basket.
2. The rebounder throws the ball high off the board and jumps for the rebound with legs spreadeagled and arms extended. The right hand should be extended so that it will grasp the top of the ball. The player pulls or rips the ball down to a position no lower than the chin.
3. After rebounding the ball, the player jumps back up for a layup. The player uses the left hand on the left side and the right hand on the right side.
4. After the layup, the player throws the ball high off the board to the opposite side and follows the same routine.

Teaching Points

1. Stress correct rebounding techniques, emphasizing going back up strong and protecting the ball while doing so.
2. Emphasize to the player that he should power-up to the basket after gaining possession of the rebound and release the ball softly against the backboard.

TIPPING DRILLS

Drill 4   Tipping Drill

1. Four players are positioned in the lane at each basket and two teammates are positioned in the outlet areas. Each player should tip the ball on the board nine times and attempt to tip it in on the tenth try. After tipping the ball into the basket, player 1 gives an outlet pass to player 3.

2. Players are to use their left hand on the left side, and their right hand on the right side.
3. Variation to this drill: the player tips nine times and then "rips" the ball down on the tenth and attempts to make an outlet pass. The next rebounder in line puts pressure on the rebounder, who tries to make the outlet pass.
4. Player 1 moves to line 3, player 3 moves to the tipping line, and player 2 becomes the rebounder.

Teaching Points

1. On successive jumps, the players should concentrate on jumping higher on each jump.
2. The player's wrists should be flexed, he should catch the ball on the finger pads of his hand, and his arm should be fully extended.
3. Players should follow through with the wrist on each shot.
4. Players should make a proper pivot and give a good outlet pass.

Drill 5 Continuous Tipping

1. One player is positioned at each basket.
2. The player tips the ball from one side of the basket to the other. The player may tip the ball five, six, eight, or ten times.

Teaching Points

1. Making a quick reaction from one side of the basket to the other.
2. One or two hands may be used.

Drill 6 Two-Player Tipping Drill

1. Two players are positioned at a basket. Depending upon the number of players on the team, three or more baskets may be used.
2. The players tip the ball nineteen times off the board and score on the twentieth tip. The player on the left side tips the ball with the left hand to the player on the right side, who makes a return tip with the right hand.
3. Players should complete three repetitions daily.

Teaching Points

1. Stress correct landing position so the player can go right back up.

2. Players should keep their wrists flexed and their arms extended.
3. Stress following through on the tip.

Drill 7   Follow the Leader—
Tip and Score—Three Players

1. Three players are positioned behind each other in the lane with player 1 in possession of the ball.
2. Player 1 tosses the ball against the backboard and moves quickly to a position behind player 3. Player 2 moves forward, times the jump, and tips the ball against the board. Player 2 then moves quickly behind player 1 so that he will be ready to tip again.
3. The drill continues with each player jumping and tipping. After each player has tipped the ball ten, fifteen, or twenty times, the last player will end the drill by tipping the ball into the basket.

Teaching Points

1. The players' hands should be in a ready position.
2. The players should move quickly to a rebound position at the end of the line and be ready to jump again.
3. There should be full extension of the arm and fingertip control of the ball.

Drill 8   Six Baskets—Two-Man Teams
Tipping the Ball at Each Basket

1. Two players are positioned at each basket (or at as many baskets as possible). Each pair has a ball.
2. The players practice tipping the ball against the backboard. They tip the ball ten times with the left hand, ten times with the right hand, and ten times with two hands. The number of tips may vary according to the coach's direction.
3. The players may also be positioned on each side of the board and may tip the ball continuously back and forth to each other.

Teaching Points

1. Stress fingertip control.
2. Stress quick reaction to get ready for another jump.
3. The coach should remind the players that each succeeding jump takes greater concentration and effort.

COMPETITIVE DRILLS

Drill 9 Rotation—Animal Drill

1. The ball is placed on the free-throw line with four offensive players positioned outside the jump circle.
2. Four defensive players are in good box-out defensive stances inside of the circle. They begin sliding to the right or left at the coach's direction. At a signal by the coach, either a whistle, yelling shot, or a clap of the hands, the defensive players must establish position and box-out the offensive player nearest them. The offensive players try to reach and touch the ball.
3. As players' skills develop, the coach can make the drill more difficult by mixing the signals or increasing the amount of time that the defensive player should hold the blockout.
4. The offensive and defensive players exchange positions.

Teaching Points

1. Defensive stance.
2. Proper footwork and shuffling movements by the defense to prevent the offensive players from reaching the ball—players should try to hold for at least three seconds.
3. Knowledge of where the ball is at all times—each player should keep the head up and eyes on the ball while maintaining the blockout position.
4. Offensive rebounding techniques such as faking and rolling off the blockout—remind the offensive rebounders to keep their hands up so that they will learn not to push and commit a foul with their hands.

Drill 10 Rotation—Triangle Rebounding

1. Two offensive players, 1 and 2, are positioned at the wing positions, while players 3, 4, and 5 are in a triangle position around the lane—one player at the high-post position and two players in the low-pivot positions at each deep block.
2. Three defensive players, X3, X4, and X5, are positioned between their offensive players and the basket.
3. The coach is positioned at the top of the circle with a ball.
4. The drill may begin with the coach either dribbling to the left or right or passing to the wing positions. As the ball moves, the defensive players must adjust their positions accordingly and be ready to block out when the shot is taken by either the coach or player 1 and 2.
5. The ball may be moved quickly from player to player before the shot is taken, so that the defensive players must move quickly to maintain proper positioning. The offensive players do not move more than one step to

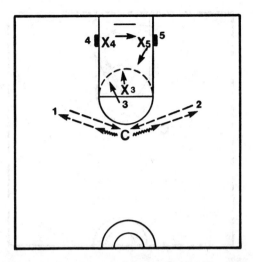

FIGURE 6-1 *Rotation–Triangle Rebounding*

the left or right as the ball is being passed but do try to present a target, set up a strong position, and be ready to receive a pass. Once the shot is taken, the offensive players try for the rebound.

6. This drill may be expanded to four-on-four and five-on-five rebounding situations.

Teaching Points

1. Defensive positioning should be emphasized as the ball is moved around the perimeter.
2. Stress aggressiveness and alertness.
3. Stress correct blockout and offensive rebounding techniques.
4. Emphasize the beginnings of team defensive principles.

Drill 11 Moving Triangle

1. The coach and a manager are positioned at the top of the key and wing positions. The offensive players (3, 4, and 5) are in a triangle position around the lane. They are guarded by defensive players X3, X4, and X5.
2. As the coach and the manager pass the ball to each other, the defensive players and offensive players rotate from one pivot position to the next. All players move either to the left or right depending upon a signal by the coach.
3. As the ball moves and the offensive players change their positions, the defensive players must adjust also.

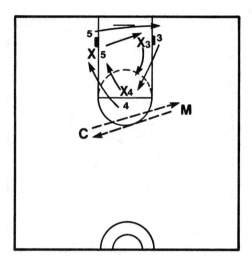

FIGURE 6-2   Moving Triangle Drill

4. The drill continues until a shot is taken. The defensive players box out and rebound, while the offensive players make moves to get the rebound.
5. The offense moves to the defense, and the defense moves to the offense as the drill continues.

Teaching Points

1. Proper footwork and lateral movement—all players should have their hands ready.
2. The rebounding takes place under game-like conditions.
3. Proper positioning on the pivot, weak-side, and help positions by the defensive rebounders.

Drill 12   One-on-One Rebounding Drill—
Block Out the Shooter

1. The players are positioned in one line at the side of the lane. The first player in line is to take a defensive position.
2. The defensive player must eventually stop three players from scoring and rebounding.
3. The defensive player gives the ball to the first offensive player; he will attempt to force the offensive player to pick up the ball or to take a bad shot. When a shot is taken, the player boxes out for the rebound.
4. As the defensive player rebounds, he or she gives an outlet pass to the next offensive player in line and approaches the offensive player quickly, under control, and in a good defensive position.

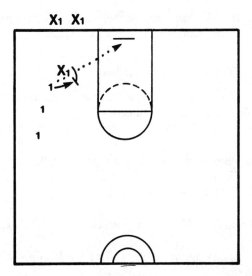

FIGURE 6-3 One-on-One Rebounding Drill—Block Out the Shooter

5. After the defensive player finishes rebounding, he or she moves to the end of the line, and the next player moves to the defensive position.
6. For conditioning and competition, have players run one lap for each basket scored on them.

Teaching Points

1. Stress defensive principles.
2. Stress rebounding techniques.
3. Emphasize aggressiveness.
4. Emphasize conditioning.

Drill 13 Two-on-One Rebound and Outlet Pass Drill

1. One player (1) is positioned in the lane as the defensive rebounder. Players X1 and X2 are offensive players. Players 2 and 3 are in the outlet pass areas.
2. Player X2 shoots the ball off the board and follows the shot.
3. Defensive player 1 boxes out offensive player X1.
4. As player 1 rebounds the ball, the offensive players X1 and X2 clamp or double-team player 1 to prevent the outlet pass.
5. If an offensive player, X1 or X2, rebounds the ball, the drill continues with a two-on-one game until the defensive player gains possession of the ball.
6. When the defensive player rebounds, he tries to make the outlet pass

very quickly. He may pass the ball as he comes down or try to penetrate the double-team with a dribble before passing.

Teaching Points

1. The coach should stress rebounding techniques, in particular that of making certain to box out an opponent.
2. Teach the rebounder to look outside toward the sidelines for the outlet pass.
3. Teach the rebounder to "break the seam" with the use of stepping-through and one dribble.
4. This drill provides a game-like situation.

Drill 14   Two-on-One—Make Three Baskets

1. A player or manager is positioned at the free-throw line with a ball in his possession.
2. Players 3, 4, and 5 are in rebounding positions along the free-throw lane. These players will attempt to rebound the ball after the shot is taken by the player at the free-throw line.
3. The player who rebounds the ball attempts to score, while the other two players try to stop the score. These players will rebound both missed and made shots; the drill continues until three baskets are scored by one player.
4. After three baskets are scored, the next three players move into the drill, or the player who scored the three baskets exchanges positions with the player at the free-throw line.

Teaching Points

1. Stress positioning to make sure a player boxes out another player on the free-throw lane.
2. The importance of getting the ball should be stressed as the main concern of this drill. The players should be aggressive and urged to make repeated efforts to gain possession of the ball.

Drill 15   Two-on-Two Rebounding
with a Basket Insert (Ring)

1. Players are positioned in two lines, one at each side of the lane. The first player in each line plays defense, and the second player becomes the offensive rebounder.
2. Player 4 starts the drill by shooting over player X4, while player X5 defends against player 5 on the weak side. Both players X4 and X5 box

out, and all four players go for the ball. They continue to rebound until someone scores or until the defense gains possession of the ball.

3. The defensive players move to the end of the line, and the offensive player moves to the defensive position against the next player in line.

Teaching Points

1. Correct footwork by the offensive player should be stressed so that he may move inside the defensive player.
2. Strong boxing-out position by the defensive player should be emphasized.
3. Mental and physical toughness should be emphasized and encouraged during the drill.

Drill 16 Woodpecker Drill

1. Two offensive players, 2 and 3, are positioned under the basket outside of the baseline facing the free-throw line. One offensive player, 1, is positioned near the midcourt area and two offensive players, 4 and 5, are positioned in the lane on either side of the basket.
2. Two defensive rebounders, X4 and X5, play between players 4 and 5 and the basket, while teammates X1 and X2 are in the outlet pass areas.
3. The ball is thrown off the backboard by the coach, and either X4 or X5 rebounds. Players 4 and 5 put pressure on the ball to prevent an outlet pass.
4. After the rebounder gains possession of the ball, players 2 and 3 try to

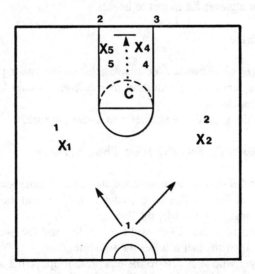

FIGURE 6-4 Woodpecker Drill

slap the ball away from the rebounder and help with a double-team on the rebounder.

5. Player 1 puts pressure on an outlet pass to player X1 or X2. Player 1 may move in either direction and has freedom of movement. This causes the pass receivers to be aware of moving to meet the pass.

Teaching Points

1. Stress boxing out.
2. Emphasize to the rebounders that they must keep the ball up to protect it from being stolen or slapped away.
3. Put pressure on the rebounder to harass the player making the outlet pass.

Drill 17   Rebounding—One-on-One

1. The players are positioned in a line at the foul line, with the first player in line becoming the defensive player and the next player in line with the ball. Players 2 and 3 are positioned in outlet areas.
2. Player 1 shoots, follows the shot, and tries to rebound the shot. If he gets the rebound, he continues to shoot until he scores.
3. Player X1 attempts to block out player 1 and gain possession of the missed shot. Player X1 makes an outlet pass to either player 2 or 3. If the score is made by player 1, player X1 will take the ball quickly out-of-bounds and make the outlet pass to either side.
4. Player 1 moves to line X1, player 2 moves to line 3, player 3 moves to line 1, and player X1 moves to line 2.

Teaching Points

1. Emphasize offensive and defensive rebounding under pressure with the defensive rebounder attempting to block the shooter before he can get moving for the ball.
2. Stress making the correct outlet pass under pressure.

Drill 18   Recover the Ball, Pick It Up, Pivot, and Drive

1. Two lines of players are positioned the same distance away from the foul line, one at the baseline on the edge of the lane and the other just inside the hash mark on the right sideline.
2. The coach rolls the ball toward the foul line and the two players go after the ball when the ball touches the foul line.
3. The player who first gets to the ball picks it up, pivots, and tries to drive to the basket.

4. The player who does not gain possession goes immediately on defense to try to prevent the drive.
5. The ball stays "alive" until the offensive player scores or the defense gains possession. The defensive player passes quickly to the coach after gaining possession. Both players move to the end of the opposite lines.

Teaching Points

1. Players should react quickly to recover the ball as well as to make the drive to the basket or go on defense.
2. The ball should be in play everywhere until the defense gains possession.

Drill 19   Two-on-One-Rebounding

1. Three lines are positioned near the foul-line area. One player is at the free-throw line and the other two players are at the wing positions.
2. The coach, who is positioned in one corner or near the baseline, shoots the ball. The first players in each line move for the rebound. The player who gains possession of the rebound tries to score immediately, while the other two players attempt to stop him from scoring.
3. If the rebounder scores, he leaves the drill and goes to the end of his line. This player is replaced by the next player in line, and the drill continues. The two players who did not score will remain until they do score or make a certain number of tries.
4. If the shot is missed, the three players continue to rebound until a score is made.

Teaching Points

1. Players should keep the action continuous.
2. Players should correct rebounding mistakes such as bringing the ball down.
3. This drill brings about strong competition. Desire and physical toughness are encouraged.

Drill 20   Power Layup

1. Two players are positioned at each basket, with each pair of players having possession of a ball.
2. Player 1 has the ball and prepares to toss the ball onto the board and over the rim toward player 2.
3. Player 2 leaps to touch the board. As player 2 returns to the floor, player 1 tosses the ball off the backboard. Player 2 jumps again, this time for the rebound, returns to the floor, and prepares to go back up for a layup.

4. After player 1 throws the ball, he or she moves across the lane to bother player 2 and prevent an easy shot from being taken. Player 1 may crowd player 2, try to block the shot, or bother player 2 in any way, so player 2 must go up strong and power the ball up to the basket.

Teaching Points

1. The rebounder must gain balance and gain a firm grip on the ball.
2. The ball should not be brought below chest level but should be in a position where the rebounder can protect it from the defense as well as be able to shoot quickly.
3. The ball should be released with a light touch after lifting it to its highest position with a power jump.

Drill 21   Five-on-Two Competitive Rebounding Drill—
Use Rebound Ring Insert

1. Players X4 and X5 are defensive rebounders who are positioned in the lane, and players 1, 2, 3, 4, and 5 are the offensive rebounders. The drill starts with the manager, who is positioned near the left or right wing positions, taking the first shot.
2. With the rebound ring or insert in place to guarantee consecutive rebounds, the players attack the board and continue to rebound until the defensive players make five rebounds. After each rebound by the defense, the ball is passed out again to the manager for the next shot.
3. After the defense has gained five rebounds, two new players are placed in the defensive positions.

Teaching Points

1. Stress continuous action by all players.
2. Defensive players must work for blockout position as well as show great determination and desire to gain control and possession of the ball.

Drill 22   Rebounding—Two-on-One

1. Players 1 and 2 are positioned at the foul line with player 2 in possession of the ball. Players 3 and 4 are in the outlet receiving areas. Player X2 plays defense against the shooter and will attempt to gain possession of the rebound.
2. Player 2 shoots the ball, and he and his teammate, player 1, attempt to gain possession of the rebound and score.
3. Player X2 bothers the shot by player 2 and then drops to a position where he can gain possession of the rebound or block out the offensive players.

He will make an outlet pass to either side after gaining possession of the ball.

4. Players 1 and 2 must place pressure on the passer, player X2, when he is attempting to make the outlet pass.
5. Player 1 goes to player 2, 2 goes to X2, X2 goes to 3, 3 goes to 4, and 4 goes to 1.

Teaching Points

1. Stress rebounding and passing against pressure.
2. Emphasize that the defensive rebounder must be aggressive.

**Drill 23   Defensive and Offensive Rebounding from
Two-on-Two—Weak-Side and Strong-Side Positions**

1. The players are positioned in two lines on either side of the lane near the wing positions, with the first player in each line playing defense.
2. The coaches, who are positioned at the guard positions, pass the ball to each other, and the defensive players move from the denial to the helping positions.
3. When either of the coaches shoots the ball, players X1 and X2 move quickly to defensive rebound positions and block out offensive players 1 and 2. This movement teaches the players to rebound on the strong side and weak side of the court while involved in game-situation movements.
4. If the defensive player recovers the ball, he or she looks to start a fast

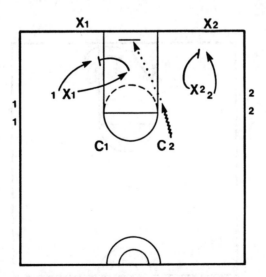

FIGURE 6-5 *Defensive and Offensive Rebounding from Two on Two—
Weak-Side and Strong-Side Positions*

break. If the offensive players recover the rebound, they try to score immediately or play a two-on-two game.

5. The defensive players move to the end of the line and the offensive players move to the defensive positions.

Teaching Points

1. The defensive player on the ball side should prevent the offensive player from getting a quick start toward the rebound.
2. The weak-side defensive player must move out to meet the offensive rebounder and prevent the offensive rebounder from getting to the ball by taking away the cutting angle.

MULTIPLAYER DRILLS

Drill 24   Three-Man Figure Eight

1. Three players are positioned across the lane. Player 1 is in the lane slightly to the right of the basket, and players 2 and 3 are on each side of the lane at the blocks.
2. Player 1 tosses the ball off the backboard and over the basket toward player 3's side and moves quickly to replace player 3.
3. Player 3 reacts to rebound the ball and tips the ball, using one or two hands, off the board and toward player 2. After tipping the ball, player 3 moves quickly to replace player 2, who reacts to rebound, tips the ball off the board toward player 1, and moves quickly to replace player 1.

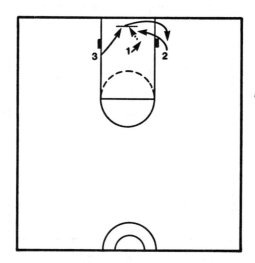

FIGURE 6-6   Three-Man Figure Eight

4. The drill continues with the players continuing to rebound or tip the ball for a specified number of times.

Teaching Points

1. Emphasize that the players should move quickly and be in a ready position with their hands up and feet moving.
2. Time the jump and tip the ball softly but firmly against the backboard.
3. This drill is a good conditioner as the players continue to move and jump. Good rebounders learn to make consecutive efforts.

Drill 25 Two-Line Rebounding and Outlet-Pass Drill

1. This drill includes all team members and would be a natural lead-up drill to a fast-break drill.
2. Two lines are formed in the free-throw lane with one player at each wing position at the foul-line extended area.
3. The first player tosses the ball against the backboard and goes up for the rebound using the correct techniques.
4. As the player comes down with the rebound, protecting the ball, he or she looks to the outside and gives a two-handed pass off the shoulder or an overhead pass to player 5. Player 1 moves to player 5's position after the pass.
5. Player 5 moves to meet the ball, pivots on the inside foot, and gives a two-handed chest or a one-handed push pass to player 4. Player 5 then takes player 4's position.
6. Player 4 makes a V-cut or an L-cut to meet the pass from player 5, receives the pass, and turns to look up court. Player 4 passes to player 2, who contin-

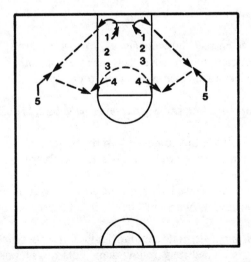

FIGURE 6-7 Two-Line Rebounding and Outlet-Pass Drill

ues the drill by tossing the ball against the board, rebounding, and making the outlet pass.

Teaching Points

1. Emphasize correct rebounding techniques including jumping with a spread-eagle position of the legs and rebounding the ball at its highest point.
2. Emphasize proper execution of the outlet pass.
3. Emphasize movement to meet the pass by the outlet man.

Drill 26 Offensive Rebounding after Individual Moves

1. Two lines are positioned on each side of the free-throw lane. The first player in the line becomes the defensive player, who will cause the rebounder to use good footwork.
2. The coach, who is positioned in the free-throw area, shoots the ball off the board. As the shot is taken, the first two offensive players (1) use reverse moves (pivots) to get around the defense to gain possession of the rebound.
3. If the offensive player gains possession of the rebound, he or she continues to shoot until scoring or until the defensive player gains possession of the ball.
4. The defensive players move to the end of their respective lines and the offensive player moves to the defense; or the coach may direct that the same defensive player remain in position for a certain number of repetitions.

Teaching Points

1. Emphasize correct footwork by the offensive players, who should work on the jab step, the crossover, and the reverse pivot.
2. Stress quickness of each movement to prevent the blockout from taking place.
3. Stress concentration and aggressiveness in getting the ball.

Drill 27 Offensive Rebounding—Follow the Shot (Use a Basket Ring or Insert)—Twelve-to-Fifteen-Foot Range

1. Two lines are stationed at each wing position with the first player in each line in possession of a ball. A basket insert is used to assure a rebound on each shot.
2. Players 1 and 2 alternate shooting jump shots or set shots. After shooting, the players immediately follow their shots to gain possession of the re-

bound. When they retrieve the ball, the players square off and shoot from that spot.

3. The number of shots is designated by the coach; after each player completes his turn, that player passes to the next player in line and moves to the opposite line.

Teaching Points

1. Stress good shooting form.
2. Players should follow the ball after shooting and gain possession of the rebound.

Drill 28 Defensive Rebounding—
Strong Side and Weak Side

1. The players are divided into two lines on either side of the foul lane. The lines are diagonal running from the foul line toward the corner.
2. As the ball is passed among the players in line 1, defensive player X1 moves with the ball from player to player. On a signal from the coach ("shoot"), the player with the ball shoots and then moves after the rebound. Player X1 must block out player 1 after attempting to bother the shot.
3. While the ball is passed in line 1, player X2 moves to the relative position on the weak side. Here player X2 blocks out player 2, who is going for the rebound because his partner in the opposite line has taken the shot.

FIGURE 6-8 *Defensive Rebounding—Strong Side and Weak Side*

4. The players may be rotated after a certain number of attempts at the rebound or after a certain period of time.

Teaching Points

1. Strong-side (ball-side) rebounding against the shooter and weak-side rebounding by both the offense and defense.
2. Defensive footwork with hands ready.
3. Reaction time, alertness, and quickness.
4. More competition may be added to the drill by having the defensive rebounder remain on defense until he gains possession of the ball.

Drill 29 Four-Line Blockout

1. The players are divided into four lines around the foul lane area. The first player in each line is on defense. A manager or player stands between two of the lines to take the shot that starts the drill.
2. The defensive players box out as the shot goes up. The coach should stress strong-side and weak-side defensive rebound positioning.
3. The offensive players make moves to rebound; if they retrieve the ball, they try to score. If the defensive players rebound, they give the ball back to the manager.
4. The players rotate positions with the defensive player moving to the end of the line and the offense going on defense.
5. After a set number of rebounds, the lines rotate to the right so that players can practice rebounding from various angles.

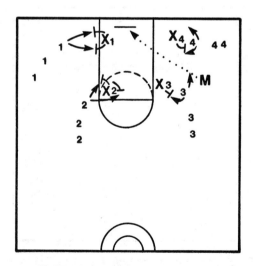

FIGURE 6-9 Four-Line Blockout

Teaching Points

1. This drill provides a game-like situation.
2. Stress offensive rebounding techniques from various positions.
3. Emphasize defensive rebounding from the strong-side and weak-side positions.

Drill 30   Five Players Try to Recover
Four Balls at the Foul Line

1. The players are positioned in groups of five along the baseline. Usually, the guards will be together and the forwards will be together . The players may be positioned with their backs to the ball or facing the ball.
2. Four balls are placed on the foul line. On a signal from the coach, the five players break quickly to try to gain possession of the four balls.
3. The four players who gain possession of the ball will play a quick game of dribble-tag in the halfcourt area. The player who does not get a ball sprints to the baseline-sideline corner position and runs a suicide sprint or performs another drill or technique that the coach may select.

Teaching Points

1. Stress competitive ideas of hustle and determination to get the ball as well as quick reaction to a signal.
2. Emphasize the ideas of concentration, alertness, and quickness.

7

Defensive Drills

INTRODUCTION

Equally important to the game of basketball is the concept of defense, both individual and team. Whatever type of defense is used, success depends on how well each player does his or her particular job.

Individual defense is concerned with correct footwork, positioning of the body, body balance, foot movement, and the use of arms, hands, and eyes. Only through individual and team drills, based on repetition and concentration, can the basic skills be developed and improved.

The drills in this chapter are progressive, beginning with basic individual techniques, moving to one-on-one situations, and progressing to team situations. The idea of defense must be sold by the coaching staff. These drills are designed to teach fundamental skills, develop attitudes, and bring about a total team concept of defense.

STANCE AND MOVEMENT

Drill 1   Gorilla Drill

1. The coach is positioned in front of the players. The coach may use a whistle, hand signal, or voice command to run the drill. All players get into defensive position, using a boxer or parallel stance with their hands ready.
2. At the coach's signal or command, the players, maintaining good defensive

stances, use shuffling and sliding movements. The players are directed to slide forward, laterally, and backwards.

3. There should be no crossing of the legs; the players are to push off the foot that is opposite to the direction in which they are going to move.

Teaching Points

1. A correct defensive stance—when this is used solely for a conditioning drill, the coach may direct the players to keep their hands above their heads for a number of minutes.
2. Players should keep knees bent (not straighten them).
3. Proper shuffling method—players should use the point-and-push method.
4. As players improve their skills, balls may be used when teaching the various moves.

Drill 2   Mirror Drill

1. The players are positioned in pairs at different parts of the court.
2. No ball is used in this drill. Offensive player 1 is to practice the jab step, rocker step, crossover step, and the fundamentals of taking a shot.
3. Defensive player X will react and move with every defensive move.
4. Player X reacts to a jab step to the right by stepping back one step with the right foot and sliding to the left in order to force the dribbler to the outside. The emphasis should be on keeping the body between the offensive player and the basket. If the offensive player jabs left, the defensive player steps back with the left foot and slides to the right.
5. When the offensive player moves to shoot, the defensive player steps up with the lead foot and extends the arm and hand nearest the ball.
6. If the offensive player takes a position with the ball over the head, the defensive player jams into him or her closely so that player 1 cannot bring the ball down to a driving position.

Teaching Points

1. Stress defensive stance—boxer or parallel.
2. Emphasize quick reaction to fakes and maintaining proper spacing.
3. Emphasize good offensive moves and fakes.

Drill 3   Group Reaction with Dribbler

1. Player 1 can dribble the ball forward, backward, or laterally.
2. The other players are to follow the movements of the dribbler.
3. Each player's hand should be in a position where one will lead the dribbler and the other will be held in front at about knee level, so as to prevent a crossover.

4. Players should keep their body between the dribbler and the basket. The defensive player should keep the head in line with the dribbling shoulder of the offensive player.
5. There should be no crossing of legs. Players are to push off the foot opposite the direction to which they are going to move.

Teaching Points

1. Stress defensive stance.
2. Emphasize hand positioning.
3. Emphasize correct shuffling—each player uses the point-and-push technique and keeps his feet moving all of the time, even when changing direction. He should not stop and remain flat-footed at any time.

PLAYING THE DRIBBLER

Drill 4   Zig-Zag

1. Player 1 dribbles in a zig-zag fashion down the court. Player X1, on defense, must keep the proper space relation to the dribbler. This depends upon the speed and ability of the players.
2. The proper defensive stance should be maintained, boxer or parallel.
3. Defensive player X1 should keep the body between the dribbler and the basket, with the head in line with dribbler's shoulder.

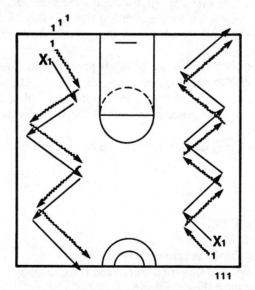

FIGURE 7-1   Zig-Zag

4. To work on shuffling, and to teach not to reach in and foul, the coach may begin the drill by having the defensive player hold his or her hands behind the back, or hold a towel with both hands behind the back, or grasp the shirt. As the defense becomes more skilled, allow the player to use hands.
5. Two methods are taught concerning the use of the hands. One is where one hand leads the dribbler and the other hand prevents the crossover dribble. The second method suggests that one hand leads, while the other attacks the ball with the hand that is closer to the dribbler.
6. The defensive player tries to make the dribbler stop or reverse direction.
7. When the coach first begins the drill, do not allow the dribbler to beat the defensive player. They are to be helping each other.

Teaching Points

1. Stress defensive stance.
2. Emphasize the correct method of shuffling so that the defensive player maintains an overplay position and forces the dribbler to change direction.
3. Stress the proper use of hands.
4. Correct dribbling technique when being pressured should be emphasized.

Drill 5   Recovery Drill

1. Players are positioned at the baseline, in two lines, at either side of the foul lane. The first player in each line is the defensive player (X1). Player X1 assumes a defensive stance in front of the offensive player (1).
2. If player 1 beats player X1, he or she continues to dribble down the court to the basket.
3. When player X1 is beaten, he or she pushes off the foot that is closest to the baseline and sprints down the court. Player X1's objective is to beat player 1 to a spot and force him to stop the dribble and pick up the ball. The players change positions and run the same drill back to the starting position.
4. The coach may use four players, two on each side of the court.

Teaching Points

1. Stress shuffling.
2. Stress defensive stance.
3. Dribbling should be emphasized.
4. Stress speed and quickness when recovering to the spot where the player will force the dribbler to stop.

**Drill 6 Roll the Ball from the Baseline—
One-on-One Drill**

1. The line under the basket plays defense, while the line at the top of the key area plays offense.
2. Player X1 rolls the ball from the baseline toward the player at the top of the free-throw circle.
3. Defensive player X1 rushes out to put pressure on the offensive player. Player X1 must stay low, with the knees bent, so as to maintain body balance as he or she comes to a stop after approaching the ball handler.
4. Player X1 challenges player 4. If player 4 dribbles, player X1 forces player 4 to the outside of the free-throw lane or forces player 4 to pick up the ball.
5. The drill continues until a score is made or until the defense gets the ball.
6. The offensive player moves to the end of line X1, and the defensive player moves to line 1.

Teaching Points

1. Speed and quickness by the defensive player when approaching the player with the ball.
2. Correct defensive stance, emphasizing the overplay technique.
3. Footwork—the defensive player must retain balance, race up to the offensive player, and be able to retreat in a position that will prevent penetration to the basket.
4. Proper dribbling technique by the offensive player.

Drill 7 Steal from Behind

1. The players are positioned in two lines as in Drill 5.
2. Player 1 drives past player X1 and tries to score at the other end of the court.
3. Player X1 pivots and begins to sprint down court following the dribbler. Player 1 should follow on the side of the dribbling hand. (For example, if the dribbler is coming down the court using his right hand, then player X1 should sprint after player 1 on the part of the court nearest the right hand.)
4. As player X1 reaches player 1, he or she attempts to tip the ball away and up the court, with the possibility of either recovering it himself or tipping it to a teammate. The tip of the ball is made with player X1's inside hand or the hand closest to the body of the dribbler, so player X1 does not reach in and foul.
5. When player X1 recovers the ball, he yells out "ball" to let teammates

know he or she has it. Player X1 begins to dribble up court, and player 1 now takes a defensive position for a one-on-one drill to the other end of the court.

Teaching Points

1. Start the drill at half speed and build toward full speed.
2. Use of hands—teach the players not to reach in and foul but to time the action for the steal just as the ball leaves the dribbler's hand.
3. Emphasize the transition game, the change from offense to defense and back to offense.

DEFENDING THE PLAYER WITH THE BALL IN THE TRIPLE-THREAT POSITION

Drill 8 One on One from the Top of the Key

1. The players are positioned in a single line at the top of the key. The first player moves to a defensive position.
2. The coach is at wing position with the ball.
3. Player X1 plays in a denial position against player 1.
4. Player 1 works to get free to receive the pass from the coach.
5. The players play one on one. At the completion of the play, the defensive player moves to the end of the line, and the offense moves to the defense.

Teaching Points

1. Shuffling and reacting to fakes.
2. Keeping body balance with the hands ready.
3. Forcing the offensive player to use his weak hand.

Drill 9 Wheeling Drill

1. Offensive player 1 is positioned one step above the foul line and in the middle of the lane. Player 1 is in possession of the ball.
2. Player X1 is positioned between offensive player 1 and the basket and is about one arm's length away from player 1.
3. Player 1 spins (pivots) on one foot and attempts to drive to the basket against player X1, who reacts and tries to prevent the drive or shot.
4. The offensive player is not allowed to drive or dribble outside of the foul lane.

Teaching Points

1. Work on quick reaction by the defensive player as the offensive player makes his turn. The defensive player should maintain correct spacing between himself and the player with the ball.
2. The offensive player should work on a variety of fakes.
3. This drill may be conducted at many baskets simultaneously.

Drill 10 Defense Against Weak-Side Forward

1. Players are positioned in one line in the forward position opposite the coach who has the ball.
2. Player X1 drops to a weak-side help position as player 1 tries to move to a position where he or she will be able to receive a pass from the coach.
3. If he receives the pass, player 1 tries to score against player X1. If he or she does not receive the pass, player 1 moves back toward the starting position and tries to make another cut toward the ball.
4. Player X1 goes to line 1, and player 1 goes to line X1.
5. After a set number of moves, the coach may move the drill to the opposite side of the floor.

Teaching Points

1. Do not allow the offensive player to receive a pass from the coach in the foul lane.
2. Correct triangle positioning by the defensive player so that he may see the ball and his man.
3. If the offensive player does receive the ball, the players go into a one-on-one drill.

DEFENDING THE PLAYER WITHOUT THE BALL

Drill 11 Denying a Weak-Side Cut from the Wing Position

1. The coach is positioned at the right forward or wing position and has a ball in his possession.
2. Player 3 is positioned at the opposite wing position while X3, the defensive player, is positioned between player 3 and the coach. Player X3's position would usually be either just inside of the foul lane (A) or at the center of the foul lane (B).
3. Player 3 tries to cut across the lane so that he may receive a pass from the coach. He or she may cut in front or behind the defensive player X3.

4. Player X3 attempts to deny the cut by offensive player 3 and prevent the offensive player from receiving the ball in scoring position.
5. If he or she is denied the pass in the lane, player 3 may return to the weak side or move to the corner on the ball side. If player 3 receives the pass in the ball-side corner, player X3 will play a one-on-one situation and try to prevent a drive to the basket.
6. If player 3 returns to the weak side, he or she may try to make another cut to receive the pass from the coach while player X3 moves to a position that will allow him to deny the cut.
7. This drill is completed by playing one-on-one whenever the offensive player receives the ball.
8. Player 3 moves to X3's position, and player X3 moves to line 3.

Teaching Points

1. Denying the cut to the ball and preventing the pass.
2. Correct positioning when playing against the weak-side wing position.
3. Defensive player X3's being aware of his man and the position of the ball at all times and maintaining the triangle ("ball-you-man") principle.

Drill 12   Deny Weak-Side Cut from the Forward (Corner) Position

1. The same rules apply to this drill as apply to Drill 11. The exception is that offensive player 3 starts in a position closer to the baseline.

Drill 13   Back-Screen Drill

1. The players are positioned in two lines: one line at the baseline between the foul lane and the sideline (line 1); the second line positioned at mid-court between the sideline and center court (line 2). The first player in each line becomes the defensive player.
2. The drill can be run at full court or at halfcourt. In this drill, forward player 2 moves to set a screen on player X1 so as to help free his teammate, player 1.
3. As player X1 is being beaten by the dribbler or is running parallel to player 1, player 2 moves up and sets a screen for player 1.
4. Player X2 must yell out "pick" in order to warn and help player X1. Player X2 can bluff and drop back, enabling player X1 to recover, or player X2 can switch to player 1. Player X1 picks up player 2 when the switch is made.
5. This drill can be run baseline to baseline with the defense and offense changing at each end. As the players' skills develop, they may play two on two and attempt to score, while using a series of back screens only.

Teaching Points

1. Defensive footwork by the person being screened and the player guarding the screener.
2. Communication between defensive players—the back man must talk.
3. Working around a pick or screen—the person being screened must antici- pate a screen, react to his teammate's warning, and then try to avoid the screen.
4. Fundamentals such as bluff and switch, where the player covering the screener shows himself to the dribbler in order to force him or her to stop or dribble in a wide arc so that the person being screened will have time to recover.

Drill 14 Six-Point Defensive Drill

1. Offensive player 1 is positioned at the foul-line extended area.
2. Player X1 is positioned in a denial position against player 1 in order to prevent a pass being made from the coach to player 1.
3. The coach has the ball and looks to make the pass to player 1.
4. Player 1 cuts toward the basket ready to receive the pass from the coach. Player X1 slides (shuffles) for two steps and maintains his denial position.
5. Player 1 continues the cut toward the basket and hesitates in the low pivot position; player X1 moves to a fronting position (move 3 in this diagram).
6. In move 4, player X1 moves to a weak-side helping position as player X1 moves across the lane to the low-pivot position.

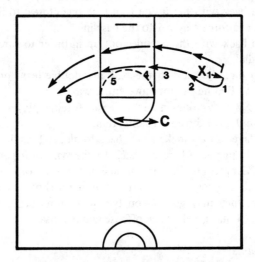

FIGURE 7-2 Six-Point Defensive Drill

7. As the coach moves across the court with the ball and player 1 starts to move toward the wing position, player X2 shuffles quickly to return to a denial position (moves 5 and 6).
8. The drill continues with the players moving from right to left, following the same procedure, until they return to their starting positions.
9. Player X1 moves to the end of the line and player 1 becomes the defensive player against player 2.

Teaching Points

1. This drill should start slowly and the tempo increase as the players master the movements and hand positioning.
2. The coach may also pass to player 1 when he is free and set up a one-on-one situation.
3. The defensive player must shuffle to keep in position between the offensive player and the ball.
4. The offensive player must keep eyes on his or her teammate and have hands ready to receive a pass.

Drill 15 Forward to Low-Pivot Drill—
Force Outside, Inside—Drop to the Ball

1. Offensive player 1 is at the forward position and player 2 is at the low-pivot area.
2. Defensive player X1 puts pressure on the passer, while player X2 tries to overplay player 2, either on the high or the low side.
3. As the pass comes to player 2, player X1 has three options: he may
   a) slide back with the inside foot (the one closest to the foul line) up in order to force player 1 to the baseline;
   b) slide back with the outside foot up in order to force player 1 to the middle;
   c) drop directly back to the ball and double-team or crowd the pivot man so that he cannot move either way.
4. Player X2 plays one-on-one defense, forcing player 2 to the baseline or the middle at the coach's direction.
5. Pivot player 2 may make a pass back to player 1; as the pass goes back to player 1, player X1 reacts back to the ball with good balance, while player X2 moves to play on one side or the other or to front player 2.
6. This drill is progressive. Start off with no shots; as the players' skills develop, they may go two on two with shots being taken. After a set number of plays, switch the offense and defense.

Teaching Points

1. Defensive footwork—the defensive player who has the ball passed directly

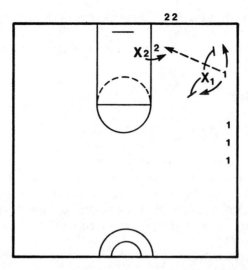

FIGURE 7-3 *Forward to Low-Pivot Drill—Force Outside, Inside—Drop to the Ball*

behind him to a pivot area must drop to a position in which to prevent the movement by the pivot man.

2. The defensive forward, player X1, should be ready to react and move out on his man on-balance when the ball is returned from the pivot to the forward. Player X1 should always know where the ball and his man are located.

3. Player X2 must work on siding and fronting the offensive pivot man and talk to his teammate player X1, telling him whether to drop back to the left or the right.

Drill 16 Two-on-One Pass—Help Against the Pivot Man

1. Two offensive players are positioned on the wing between the foul-line extended area and the baseline, and in the low-pivot area.

2. Player X1 is in a position to defend against the wing man. As the wing man passes the ball to the pivot man, defensive player X1 drops off the pivot and moves toward the ball in order to help on the pivot man. Player X1 should not turn his back on the wing man as he or she makes this move but should know where the ball and his man are located at all times.

3. As the pivot man returns the ball to the wing man, player X1 must recover to a good defensive position against player 4. Player X1 can practice jamming the offensive player if he or she brings the ball up over the head in order to prevent a shot, pass, or drive, forcing the offensive player to turn his back).

4. This drill usually lasts for sixty seconds as the ball is passed. The three players rotate positions.
5. The drill may be run at all available baskets; both sides of the lane should be used.

Teaching Points

1. Stress defensive stance and footwork.
2. The help-and-recover movement with correct shuffling when a ball is passed over the head of the defender, as well as the on-balance but aggressive approach to the wing man when the ball is passed out from the pivot—the defensive player should be reminded to approach the player with the ball with the hands in a position to bother a pass to the pivot as well as to be in a position to prevent a drive to the basket.

Drill 17 Post Pick Drill

1. Line 1 is positioned as indicated, with the first player in the line becoming player X1.
2. Two offensive players (3 and 4) are positioned at each corner of the foul line. They will not touch the ball but will be responsible for setting picks for the dribbler, player 1.
3. Player X1 is in a good stance ready to defend against player 1, who becomes the dribbler. Player X1 slides right or left according to the movement of the dribbler. When driven into a pick, player X1 must swing his lead foot out and around the pick, straightening up slightly.

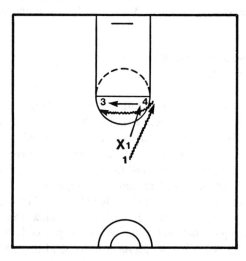

FIGURE 7-4 Post Pick Drill

As he does so, player X1 must fight over at least two picks, using his hands to find the picks and listening to his teammates' warning.

4. Player 1 must drive player X1 into a pick or picks by using the crossover or reverse dribbles.
5. After two picks are used, player 2 attempts to score from a drive or a jump shot, and both players stay in the one-on-one situation until someone scores.
6. The post men remain in the same positions, player X1 moves to the end of line 1, and the dribbler, player 1, moves to defend against the next player in line 1.

Teaching Points

1. Correct defensive stance and shuffle movement against the dribbler should be emphasized.
2. Aggressiveness when fighting over picks—the defensive player should not turn the head to look for picks; he or she should anticipate them when the dribbler moves sideways and make only quick glances out of the corner of his eye.
3. Stress use of hands.
4. Emphasize the use of proper dribbling technique when trying to drive the defensive player into a pick.
5. The post players who are setting the screens should talk and warn the defensive player that a pick is being set.
6. Defensive players may be added to defend against offensive players 3 and 4.

Drill 18 Guard Helps After a Pass
to the Post

1. The players are positioned in two lines. Line 1 is at the left (or right) guard position, and line 5 is on the baseline. The first player in line 5 is on offense, and the second player is on defense. The first player in line 1 becomes player X1, the defender.
2. Player 1 passes to player 5, who is positioned at the high post.
3. Defensive guard X1 drops to the side of the post to force the post man to turn to the inside. This move will also force player 1 to cut to the inside.
4. Player X1 goes to line 1, player 1 goes to line X1, player X5 goes to line 5, and player 5 goes to line X5.

Teaching Points

1. Stress a quick move by the defensive guard to the side position of the post as soon as the ball is passed over the head or behind him.
2. The defensive post man must talk and help player X1.

Drill 19   Five-Spot Pick Drill
(Over the Top or Slide Through)

1. Player X1 establishes a defensive stance and defends against a dribbler (6), who is at the top of the key position.
2. Offensive player 6 dribbles player X1 into a pick, either to the left or the right. The offensive player may use crossover and reverse dribbles and move the defensive player into many screens (picks) which are being set at different positions on either of the free-throw lanes.
3. Player X1 slides to the right or the left. When he reaches a pick, he extends the lead foot out and around the pick, while straightening up slightly. Each player must fight over the five picks. The defensive player must fight over the picks after being warned by teammates that a pick is being made. The players setting the picks do the talking.
4. After completing the movements against the screens, the dribbler takes the ball to the corner and plays a one-on-one game against player X1.

Teaching Points

1. Correct defensive stance and shuffling movements should be emphasized.
2. Stress aggressiveness by the defensive players who must fight over the picks.
3. Use of hands—players should find picks with their hands, not by turning the head and anticipating that there is a pick when the offensive player dribbles to the side.
4. Emphasize correct dribbling technique.

Drill 20   Reaction to the Ball After the Offensive
Player Passes the Ball (Guard to Guard)

1. Offensive players 1 and 2 are positioned at the foul-line extended area.
2. Players X1 and X2 defend against players 1 and 2.
3. Player 2 passes to player 1, fakes a cut to the basket, and steps back toward the ball ready for a return pass from player 1.
4. As player 2 passes to player 1, player X1 reacts quickly in the direction of the pass and slightly back toward the basket. This move by the defense prevents player 2 from cutting between the ball and player X2.
5. When player 1 returns the ball to player 2, player X1 reacts off and toward the ball in order to defend against a cut by player 1 or a drive into the middle by player 2.
6. The players remain in these positions and move the ball quickly back and forth to each other, with no other movement allowed until the coach changes the drill.
7. Player 1 moves to line 2, player 2 moves to line X2, player X2 moves to line X1, and player X1 moves to line 1.

Teaching Points

1. Emphasize quick reaction to helping positions.
2. Players should prevent a cut between the ball and the defensive player.
3. Stress the use of perimeter passing only.

Drill 21   Hedge or Bluff Drill

1. The players are positioned in two lines at the guard and forward positions.
2. Player 1 dribbles the ball toward his teammate player 2, who sets a screen for him.
3. Defensive player X1 slides with player 1 into the pick. Defensive player X2 slides with player 2 as he sets the pick. Player X2 should play hard defense to force player 2 to set the pick higher and more outside than he wants. Player X2 should yell out "pick left" or "pick right," depending on the movement.
4. Player X1 slides toward the pick, trying to get over the top.
5. Player X2 stays on the outside or sideline side of the pick with the outside foot extended forward and his outside hand extended forward about waist height. Player X2 attempts to force player 1 to pick up the ball.
6. If player X1 gets over the top of the screen, player X1 stays with player 1 and the drill continues, with player 1 dribbling back over player 2's screen.
7. Continue picks and hedges until there is a score or until the defense gains possession of the ball.
8. The offense goes to the defense, and the next two players in line go on offense.

Teaching Points

1. Correct footwork and shuffling procedure.
2. Communication between players.
3. Being aggressive on going over the top and making the hedge move—the player who hedges must be sure that he is in a position to force the dribbler to go wide or to stop.

Drill 22   High Pivot and Single Guard— Force Inside or Outside

1. Offensive player 1 plays the guard position and player 2 plays the high-pivot position at the free-throw line. Player X1 guards player 1 and player X2 guards player 2.
2. Player 1 passes to player 2 and attempts to cut to the left. Defensive player

X1 slides in order to block off the path of player 1, forcing player 1 to go to the outside.

3. Another way is to have defensive player X1 play with the outside foot up and force offensive player 1 to take an outside path.
4. Defensive player 2 should overplay until player 2 receives the pass. Once the pass comes to player 2, player X2 plays accordingly: if 2 is a good shooter, jamming him; if not, dropping off slightly and helping against the cutter.
5. Once the pass goes to player 2, complete the drill as a two-on-two game.
6. After a score or defensive rebound, the next players in each line move to the offensive positions, and the offensive players move to defense. The defensive players go to the end of the lines.

Teaching Points

1. Stress how to play against the high-pivot position.
2. Emphasize good footwork and body balance to force the guard inside or outside.
3. Stress communication between defensive players.

Drill 23   Weak-Side Cut from the Guard and Forward Positions (Two-on-Two Situation)

1. Player 1 is positioned at the guard position and player 3 is the weak-side forward.
2. Players X1 and X3 defend against the cut being made toward the lane by players 1 and 3.
3. The coach has the ball and will attempt to make the pass either to player 1 or 3.
4. Player 1 makes the cut first; player X1 tries to deny the cut toward the ball and force player 1 to cut behind him.
5. Just as player 1 begins the cut, player 3 starts to move out toward the foul line so as to get into a position to make a cut into the lane. Player X3 must adjust his position so that he will deny player 3's cut toward the ball and prevent the pass from being made to player 3.
6. After player 1 does not receive a pass from the coach, he moves to the position originally occupied by player 3 and prepares himself to make another cut to the ball after player 3 has made a cut.
7. Player 3 returns to the original position and prepares to make another cut.
8. Players X1 and X3 continue to work on their weak-side defense.
9. If a pass is successful to either player 1 or 3, that player may shoot or make a play to a teammate and start a two-on-two game.
10. The coach may have the players make a certain number of cuts, set a time limit for each set of players (e.g., twenty or thirty seconds), or

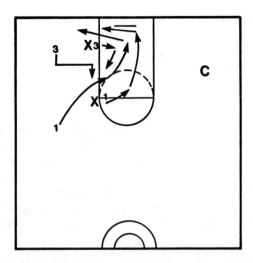

FIGURE 7-5 *Weak-Side Cut from the Guard and Forward Positions (Two-on-Two Situation)*

he may shoot the ball and have the players rebound and block out as they would in a game situation.

11. Player 1 goes to line X1, player X1 goes to line 1, player 3 goes to line X3, and player X3 goes to line 3.

Teaching Points

1. Stress correct timing of the cuts.
2. Stress correct positioning, movement, talk, and help by the defensive players.
3. Emphasize proper hand position and the maintaining of an alert defensive position by the defense as the offense cuts away from the ball.
4. The defensive players should be instructed not to chase the offensive player as he moves away from the ball and to maintain the correct angle and helping position.

Note: This drill may also be expanded to include the following:

1. A second coach (or manager) is added to the drill. He is positioned at the forward position on the opposite side of the court from the coach who has the ball.
2. As the players are cutting and the defense is taking away the cuts, coach 1 may pass the ball across the court to coach 2. This causes the defensive players to react quickly and move to positions between the player they are covering and the ball.

3. The drill continues in the same manner for a predetermined number of times.

Drill 24 Weak-Side Help and Take the Charge

1. The coach is positioned near the top of the key and has possession of the ball.
2. Player 1 is positioned at the wing position on the ball side. Player X1 plays against player 1 and denies the pass from the coach to player 1.
3. Player 2 is positioned on the weak side in the forward position, while player X2 plays defense on the weak side against player 2.
4. Because player 1 is being overplayed and denied the pass by player X1, he cuts behind him to the basket and receives a pass from the coach. Player 1 then drives to the basket to attempt a layup shot.
5. As player 1 receives the pass, player X2 moves across the lane to a position that will bring him into the path of player 1, who is driving for the layup. Player X2 will take a charge or force player 1 to stop his drive to the basket.
6. Player X1 recovers from an overplay position and moves quickly to the weak side to defend against offensive player 2, who could receive a pass from player 1 or rebound when a shot is taken.
7. Player 1 moves to line X1, player X1 moves to line 2, player 2 moves to line X2, and player X2 moves to line 1.

Teaching Points

1. Player X2 must react so that he gets to the helping position on time to take the charge legally.

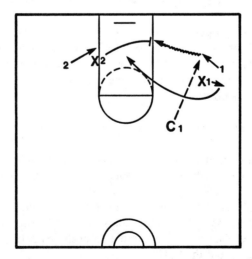

FIGURE 7-6 Weak-Side Help and Take the Charge

2. Player X1 recovers to the help position on the weak side.
3. Stress a strong denial by player X1.
4. A second coach or manager may be added at a position opposite coach (1) so that the ball may be shifted from side to side.

Drill 25   Deny the Flash Post and Roll to the Pivot

1. The coach and player 2 each have a basketball.
2. Player 1 starts in the offensive forward position.
3. Player X1 is in a defensive help position in the lane and away from the ball. Player X1 is in a position to help against a penetrating drive by either the coach or player 2, or, in this situation, to defend against a pass to player 1, who cuts toward the ball from the weak side.
4. As player 1 cuts across the lane, player X1 tries to deny the cut by blocking his path. Player X1 deflects the pass being made to player 1 by the coach.
5. As player X1 deflects the pass, player 1 rolls down the lane, looking to receive a pass from player 2. Player X1 must move quickly to a position to either deny or deflect player 2's pass to player 1.
6. Player 2 goes to line 1, player 1 goes to line X1, and player X1 goes to line 2.

Teaching Points

1. Correct positioning by player X1 on the weak side of the court.
2. Proper denial movement against the cut from the weak side.
3. Proper stance when fronting a player who is in the low-pivot position.

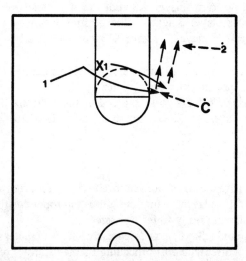

FIGURE 7-7   Deny the Flash Post and Roll to the Pivot

4. The defensive player's being aware of man and ball at all times and keeping the body between man and the ball.

Drill 26 Denial Drill Continuation

1. This drill is a continuation of Drill 25.
2. The drill continues if the pass to player 1 from player 2 is denied (prevented).
3. Player 2 makes a return pass to the coach, and player 1 slides up the lane, ready to receive the pass from the coach.
4. Player X1 moves up the lane, trying to deny player 1 from receiving the pass.
5. If player 1 is unable to receive a pass from the coach, he cuts away from the ball to his starting position on the weak side. Player X1 should use the correct technique and footwork while sliding to the weak-side defensive position.

Drill 27 Three on Three—Defense Slides Through
(or Switches) During Three-Man Weave

1. The players are positioned in three lines at the top of the key and wing positions. The first three players in each line become the defensive players.
2. Player 1 dribbles to the right and makes a handoff pass to player 3. Player X1 slides (shuffles) in the direction that the dribbler is moving. Player X1 sees player X3 out of the corner of his eye or may also touch player X3 with his extended hand. Player X1 steps back and allows player X3 to slide between him and player 1, who makes the handoff to player 3.
3. Player 3 continues the drill by dribbling toward player 2, who is at the left wing position. Player X3 slides across while defending against the dribbler. As player 3 reaches the position where he or she will make a handoff pass to player 2, player X3 steps back to allow player X2 to slide through.
4. The drill continues until each defensive player has had the chance to slide through a specified number of times.
5. The defensive players go to the end of the offensive line, and the three offensive players (1, 2, 3) move to the defensive positions.

Teaching Points

1. The defensive players should shuffle using correct footwork.
2. The defensive player's hands should be in proper position when guarding the dribbler and ready to feel for screens.
3. Players should talk when on defense and help teammates to slide through.
4. Stress the correct handoff procedure by the offensive players.

Drill 28 Reaction to the Ball After the Offensive Players Pass the Ball (Guard-Guard-Forward)

1. Same movements as in Drill 20, with additional players X3 and 3.
2. At the end of the drill, the defensive players move to the end of their respective lines and the offensive players move to defense.
3. The teaching points to be stressed are the same as in Drill 20.

Drill 29 Denial and Helping Positions

1. The coach has the ball and is positioned near the top of the key.
2. Offensive players 1 and 2 are positioned at the foul-line extended area.
3. Players X1 and X2 are defensive players.
4. The coach may move right (move A) or left (move B). If he starts to the right, player X1 moves into a strong denial position against player 1; player X2 drops off and away from player 2, as the coach moves to the right, and moves into a helping position.
5. If the coach moves to the left, player X2 moves to deny the pass to player 2, and player X1 drops off to a helping position.
6. If the coach passes successfully to one of the players, players 1 and 2 will attempt to score in a two-on-two game. The ball may also be returned to the coach to begin the drill again.
7. If the coach is able to make the pass to an offensive player who is cutting behind the defensive player toward the basket, the opposite defensive player moves to a position to take the charge. (See Drill 30.)

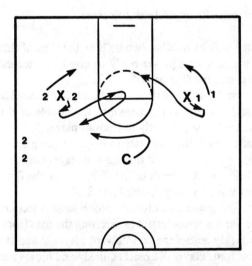

FIGURE 7-8 Denial and Helping Positions

Teaching Points

1. Stress denial position.
2. Stress weak-side helping position.
3. Players should make a quick recovery to their own man after helping to prevent penetration by the player their teammate is guarding.

Drill 30   Denial and Helping Positions—
Help and Recover

1. The players are positioned in two lines as in Drill 33, with the first player in each line moving to the defense.
2. In this situation, the coach makes a penetrating dribble, causing the two defensive players, X1 and X2, to react to shut off the drive.
3. The coach passes either to player 1 or 2, and the two-on-two game begins as the defense reacts and recovers to correct their defensive positions.
4. The defensive player moves to the end of the line and the offensive player moves to the defense.

Teaching Points

1. Players should stop the penetrating dribble.
2. Players should recover to defensive positions against the players they are defending.
3. The defensive player who is guarding the player without the ball must be aware of helping against a drive into the middle as well as of preventing a cut into the middle of the lane by the player he is guarding.

Drill 31   Defensive Pivot—Help and Recover

1. The coach will be holding two balls at the start of this drill (or will have a team manager or a player ready to give him a second ball immediately after he passes the first ball).
2. Players 1 and 2 are positioned at the foul-line extended area (wing positions), and player 3 is positioned at the middle of the foul lane. Player X1 positions himself directly in front of player 3.
3. The coach makes the first pass to player 1 (or player 2). As this pass is made, player 3 cuts toward the ball and stays ready to receive a pass from player 1. Player X1 reacts in the direction of the first pass and attempts to deflect this pass away from player 3.
4. After the first pass is deflected, the coach passes a second ball to player 2.
5. When player 3 is unsuccessful in receiving the pass from player 1, player 3 moves quickly across the lane toward player 2 and is ready to receive a pass from him. Player X1 reacts quickly and moves across the lane to try to get into a position to deny or deflect the pass to player 3.

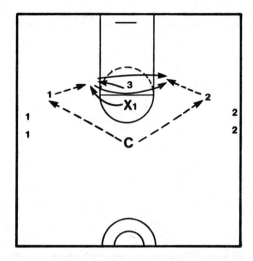

FIGURE 7-9 *Defensive Pivot—Help and Recover*

6. If player 3 does receive the pass, player X1 must play against player 3 in a one-on-one game situation. They play until a score is made or until the defense gains possession.
7. Player X1 goes to line 1, player 3 goes to line X1, player 1 goes to line 2, and player 2 goes to line 3.

Teaching Points

1. Stress a strong cut to the ball by the offensive pivot man.
2. Stress a quick reaction and recovery by the defensive post player.
3. This drill may be used for all team members or may be used only for the big men.

Drill 32 Guarding the Cutter from the Weak Side
Who Cuts off the High-Pivot Screen

1. Players are positioned as indicated. Player X1 defends against the cutting guard, player 1, and player X5 defends against the offensive player 5.
2. Player 1 passes to player 2, who passes to player 3. As the pass is made from player 2 to player 3, player 1 tries to cut over the top of a block (screen) by player 5. Player X1 tries to prevent player 1 from cutting between X1 and the ball and tries to force player 1 to go behind the screen and away from a direct pass possibility.
3. Player X5 must talk and help player X1 to get "over the top" of the screen.
4. Player X1 goes to line 3, player 3 goes to line 2, player 2 goes to line 1,

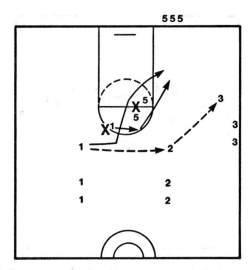

FIGURE 7-10 Guarding the Cutter from the Weak Side Who Cuts Off the High-Pivot Screen

player 1 goes to line X1, player 5 goes to the end of line 5, and player X5 moves to line 5.

Teaching Point

1. Do not allow the cutter to drive the defensive player into a screen or to cut between the defensive player and the ball. The defensive player tries to remain on the ball side of the post.

Drill 33 Denial, Weak-Side Help, Take the Charge

1. The players are positioned in two lines on each side of the court. The first player in each line moves to a defensive position (X1 and X2) and defends against the first player in line.
2. Two coaches are positioned as indicated, and one ball is used.
3. Coach 1 passes the ball to coach 2 and player X2 moves into a position to deny a pass from coach 2 to offensive player 2, who tries to get free for the pass. As the pass is made from coach 1 to coach 2, defensive player X1 moves to a weak-side helping position in the lane.
4. Player 2 makes a reverse "back door" cut toward the basket and receives a pass from the coach. Player X1 moves quickly to a position on the baseline, takes the charge and stops player 2's penetration. Player X2 must recover and switch to defend against offensive player 1.
5. The drill may continue with the ball being exchanged between the coaches,

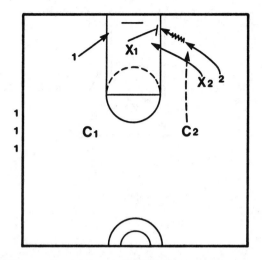

FIGURE 7-11 Denial, Weak-Side Help, Take the Charge

therefore causing players X1 and X2 to exchange responsibilities as the ball moves.

6. The drill continues until the defense recovers the ball or takes the charge. The offense continues to try to score in a two-on-two game.
7. The defensive players move to the end of their lines, and the offensive player moves to play defense against the next player in line.

Teaching Points

1. Denial of the pass on the ball (strong) side.
2. Correct angles for the player in the weak-side helping position.
3. Taking the charge from directly in front of the offensive player, who is driving.
4. Being ready to stop a penetrating drive by the coach and then recovering to one's own man.
5. Offensive players should work on the timing needed to make a successful reverse cut.

HELP-RECOVER DRILLS

Drill 34 Two-on-Two Help-Recover at Guard
Positions Against the Jump Shooter

1. Player 2 passes to player 1, and tries to cut to the basket. Player X2 drops off and toward the ball to force player 2 to cut behind him or her.

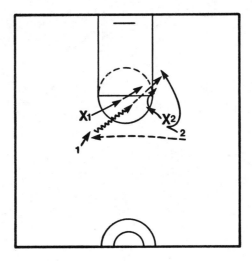

FIGURE 7-12   Two-on-Two Help-Recover at Guard Positions against the Jump Shooter

Having been denied an inside cut toward the basket, player 2 moves to the foul line extended area position.

2. Player X2, after having denied player 2 a cut to the basket, is also in position to help teammate, player X1, when offensive player 1 makes a drive into the middle and toward the basket.

3. Offensive player 1 starts a drive into the middle but is forced to stop by player X2. Player 1 passes to player 2, who is in a position ready to receive the pass and shoots a jump shot.

4. Player X2, after helping player X1, recovers quickly to a position between player 2 and the basket and attempts to bother the shot by player 2.

5. This drill may also be run by adding a second option for player 2; that is, he may shoot or drive, and player X2 must defend against both offensive moves.

6. Player 1 goes to line 2, player 2 goes to line X2, player X2 goes to line X1, and player X1 goes to line 1.

Teaching Points

1. Quick movement by player X2 into a helping position by using proper shuffling movements and readiness to react back toward offensive player 2 when the pass is made.

2. Correct procedure for moving off and toward the ball after the man a player is guarding has passed the ball.

Drill 35 Two-on-Two Help-Recover from Guard-Forward Positions

1. Same responsibilities and movements as in Drill 34.

Teaching Points

1. Recovery by player X2 to prevent a baseline drive by player 2, who has received the pass from player 1. Player X1 must get back to a helping position to deny a drive into the middle when player X2 takes away the baseline drive.

Drill 36 Two-on-Two Help-Recover Against the Driver

1. The players are positioned in two lines at the guard positions as indicated in Drill 34.
2. Player 2 has the ball and starts the drill by passing to player 1. As player 2 passes the ball, player X2 moves toward the direction of the pass and toward the basket so that he or she will be in a helping position against player 1. Player 1 dribbles toward the middle but is forced to stop by player X2. As player 1 starts the drive toward the middle, player 2 moves to a position at the corner of the lane and is ready for a pass from player 1.
3. Player X2 bluffs toward player 1, forcing player 1 to stop the dribble and make a pass to player 2. As player 1 stops the dribble and picks up the ball, player X2 moves quickly back to defend against player 2. Player X1 drops to a helping position after player 1 makes the pass. Player X1 is then ready to prevent a penetrating move by player 2 and recover the ball back for 1, who has moved to the left side of the lane after passing to player 2.
4. This drill may continue as a two-on-two game with the defensive players concentrating on the help-and-recover technique. The coach may control the movement so that there is only a designated number of exchanges.

Teaching Points

1. Continuous movement by the defensive players from the helping position to the recovery position.
2. Correct bluffing procedure and proper positioning so that the dribbler must stop his penetration and make a pass.

Drill 37 Two-on-Two Recovery—Full Court

1. Two lines are positioned at the baseline. The first two players move to the defense, and the second players play offense. Player 1 starts with the ball in his possession.

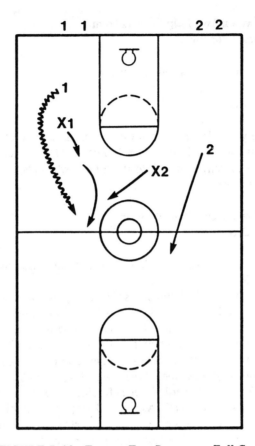

FIGURE 7-13 *Two-on-Two Recovery—Full Court*

2. Defensive player X1 is beaten by the dribbler down court. As player 1 starts to dribble past player X1, player X2 moves more toward the ball from the helping position, so that he or she will be in a position to cause the dribbler to stop or change direction.

3. There are two ways to carry out this drill. First, player X2 may go to a certain point to "bluff" at the dribbler, enabling player X1 to recover and get back into position. Secondly, player X2 may "switch" to defend against player 1. If player 2 does switch, player X1 immediately moves to pick up player 2, shutting down the passing lane as well as staying ready to help on the weak side.

4. The drill continues in a two-on-two game, with an attempt to score by the offense.

5. After a score, offense goes on defense, and defense on offense. If the defensive players intercept or recover the ball, they break quickly on offense.

Teaching Points

1. Correct defensive stance.
2. Communication on defense.
3. Help-and-recovery techniques.
4. Aggressiveness and hustle on defense.
5. Dribbling and passing.

Drill 38 Help and Recover by the Forward and Guard

1. The players are positioned in three lines as indicated, with the first two players in lines 1 and 2 moving to defensive positions. Player 3 will not have a defensive player against him and will remain there for a set number of plays before moving to a defensive line.
2. The coach (or manager) has possession of the ball to start the drill.
3. The coach makes a pass to player 3, who immediately drives to the basket.
4. On the pass to player 3, player X2 moves quickly across the lane from the weak-side helping position (A) and causes player 3 to stop the penetration to the basket. Player X1 moves from the defensive position at the foul-line area to the weak side (B) in order to block out player 2 if player 3 shoots. Player X1 is also in a position to prevent a pass across the lane from player 3 to player 2.
5. When player 3 is stopped, he or she may either shoot or pass to player 1. If the pass is made to player 1 from player 3, player X1 recovers to play against player 1, and player X2 moves quickly to a helping position, ready to react to cover player 2.

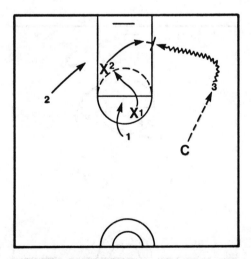

FIGURE 7-14 Help and Recover by the Forward and Guard

6. When player 3's drive is stopped by player X2, player 3 makes a quick pass to the foul-line area to player 1.
7. Player X1 reacts quickly and returns to defend against offensive player 1. Player X2 moves quickly across the lane to defend against player 2, who may receive a pass from player 1 or move for an offensive rebound if player 1 shoots.

Teaching Points

1. Shutting off the drive by player 3 and recovering to the offensive players.
2. Blocking out and rebounding aggressively when the shot is taken.

Drill 39   Help and Recover by Forward and Guard—
Alternate to Drill 38—Add a Third Defensive Player

1. A third defensive player may be added to defend against player 3 after player 3 returns the pass to player 1.
2. Player X3 has the responsibility to deny a return pass to player 3 and also to block player 3 away from the offensive rebound.

Drill 40   Help and Recover—Three-on-Three

1. Defensive player X3 and offensive player 3 are added to the two-on-two drill.
2. Player 2, after receiving a pass from player 1, starts a drive to the basket.
3. Player X3 moves to a helping position and forces player 2 to stop the

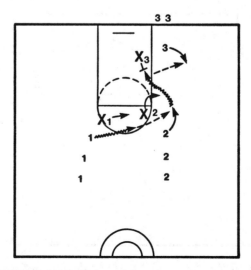

FIGURE 7-15   Help and Recover—Three on Three

drive and make a pass to offensive player 3, who has stepped away from the side of the lane.
4. After the pass is made from player 2 to player 3, player X3 must recover to defend against player 3, who is in a position to shoot or drive.
5. Players X2 and X1 make the correct movements to defensive helping positions.

Teaching Point

1. These are the same as shown in the previous help-and-recover drills.

Drill 41   Four-on-Four Shell Drill

1. The players are positioned in four lines as indicated.
2. The defensive players move and adjust their positions as the ball is passed around the perimeter.
3. After players learn the reaction to the ball's movement, the drill may increase in tempo. The offensive players may also be allowed to make a variety of moves.
4. Four new players may replace the four defensive players and the four offensive players will become the defenders after a series of passes and moves or after a set period of time.

Teaching Points

1. The coach must stress good defensive balance and footwork.
2. Players should always know where the ball is.

FIGURE 7-16 *Four-on-Four Shell Drill*

3. The emphasis should be placed on teamwork, such as the need for players to help on the weak side.

Drill 42 Four-on-Four Support Drill with Weak-Side Help

1. Players are positioned in groups of four as in Drill 41—two guards and two forwards with defensive players guarding each offensive player.
2. Player 2 passes to player 1, who passes to player 3. As the passes are made, the defensive players drop off and toward the ball into helping positions. Player X3 moves to deny the pass to player 3 but does not succeed.
3. Player 3 drives hard to the basket along the baseline as player X4 moves from the weak-side forward position to stop player 3's drive or takes a charge.
4. Players X1, X2, and X3 collapse toward the basket to jam the middle, and player X2 moves into a position to defend against a pass from player 3 to player 4 across the baseline.
5. The offensive team of four players moves to the defense. The defensive team moves to the end of the lines and rotates positions. Player 1 goes to line 2, player 2 goes to line 4, player 4 goes to line 3, and player 3 goes to line 1.

Teaching Points

1. The weak-side forward must move quickly to the helping position.
2. All defensive players must drop to helping positions and should be moving as the ball moves.
3. There should not be penetration of any kind into the middle.

PIVOT DRILLS

Drill 43 Defending the Moving Pivot
(Pass Around the Perimeter)

1. Player X5 is positioned in front of the offensive pivot, player 5, and the coach or player 4 has the ball.
2. Other players (4, 3, 2, 6) and the coach fill the positions indicated in the diagram.
3. The ball is passed around the perimeter. As he or she receives the ball, each offensive player looks inside and tries to pass to offensive player 5.
4. Player X5 moves quickly to maintain a position between player 5 and the ball so that he may discourage or prevent a pass from being made to player 5.
5. Players 5 and X5 move along the edges of the foul lane and in the lane.

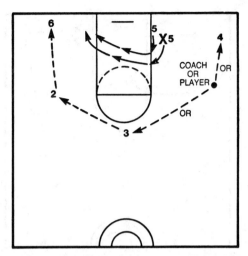

FIGURE 7-17 *Defending the Moving Pivot (Pass around the Perimeter)*

6. If the pass is successful and player 5 is able to shoot, both players rebound.
7. Rotate all forwards and pivot players to different positions in this drill.

Teaching Point

1. Correct hand-and-foot positions by the defensive pivot man should be emphasized. Players should maintain the denial position as long as possible.

**Drill 44 Defending the Moving Pivot
with the Addition of Weak-Side Help**

1. Using the same procedure as in Drill 43, the only additional movements are the moves to the helping positions by the players on the weak side.
2. Player X5 plays in front of offensive player 5 when the ball is passed to player 4. Player X5 knows that he will have help from his teammates, so he can work very hard to prevent a pass from player 4 to player 5.
3. As the ball is passed to player 4, player 6 moves into the lane to defend against a pass from player 4 to player 5 over the head of player X5. Player 2 may also drop into a helping position in the lane.
4. If the ball is passed to the opposite side of the court to player 6, then player 4 drops into the lane to help the defensive pivot man from the weak side.

Teaching Points

1. Correct positioning by the players on the weak side of the court should be emphasized.

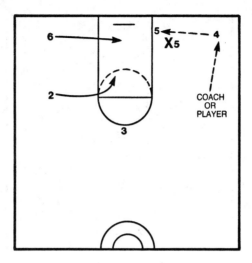

FIGURE 7-18   Defending the Moving Pivot with the Addition of Weak-Side Help

2. The defensive player on the weak side should talk—tell his teammate, player X5, that he is in a position to help him.
3. Stress to the defensive pivot player that he should not worry about a ball being thrown over his head because he will have help.

TWO-ON-TWO DRILLS

Drill 45   Double-Team from Pass-and-Go-Away Movement

1. This drill can be run from the guard positions or the guard-forward positions.
2. Player 1 passes to player 2 and cuts away from the ball.
3. Player X1 takes one step back and then springs to the ball to double-team player 2.
4. Player X2 steps up to the ball with his outside foot up, to force player 2 to the middle.
5. A variation is to have player 2 start to dribble to the right with player X2 using a lateral movement to the outside, so that player 2 must reverse direction and turn his back on player X1, who moves to set up a double team.
6. The offense moves to the defense, and the defensive player moves to the end of the offensive line.

Teaching Points

1. Stress forcing the ball into the middle.
2. Player X1 must react quickly to the ball. As player X1 approaches 2, he or she should have hands up in order to make passing difficult.

Drill 46 Two-on-Two–Zig-Zag, Help and Recover–Full Court

1. Player 1 dribbles down court with defensive player X1 attempting to force him to stop or change direction. Player X1 should not reach in but should try to force the dribbler to change direction with body position.

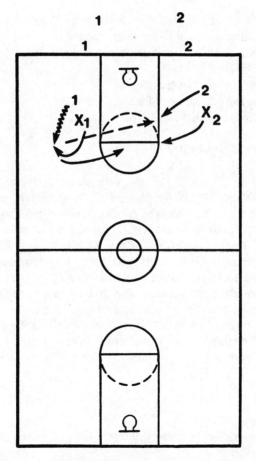

FIGURE 7-19 *Two-on-Two–Zig-Zag–Help and Recover–Full Court*

2. Defensive player X2 drops off and toward the ball to be in a position to help if the offensive player tries to move to the middle of the court.
3. If offensive player 1 picks up the ball, defensive player X1 should crowd him to prevent a good pass from being made. As this happens, defensive player X2 recovers to his man in a denial position.
4. If offensive player 2 receives a pass, defensive player X2 recovers and maintains a good defensive position, forcing the player to the outside. As this happens, player 1 drops off and toward the ball.
5. An alternate to this drill is to have the weak-side player play complete denial at all times.
6. When the drill reaches the other end of the court, the defense moves to offense and the offense moves to defense.

Teaching Points

1. Defensive techniques should be stressed—good balance, and strong overplay position on the dribbler, with one hand extended to make passing and dribbling difficult and the other hand ready to prevent the crossover dribble.
2. Stress help-and-recover techniques.
3. Dribbling and passing should be emphasized.
4. Stress communication on defense.

Drill 47   Two-on-One Drill—Full Court

1. Players 1 and 2 are on offense, with player 2 staying parallel with or slightly behind the dribbler, player 1, ready to receive a pass from him.
2. Defensive player X1 maintains good defensive positioning, trying to force the dribbler to use the weak hand or to pick up the ball.
3. If player 1 passes to player 2, player X1 may move to a help-and-recover position or into a denial position on player 1, as designated by the coach.
4. If player 1 receives a return pass from player 2, player X1 returns to the one-on-one defensive position. The drill continues the full length of the court and ends with an attempted shot by player 1.
5. The drill becomes a two-on-one rebounding drill until someone scores.
6. The drill continues with the offensive player 1 moving to the defense and defensive player X1 moving to offense. Player 2 remains in the same position.

Teaching Points

1. Good one-on-one defensive techniques using the overplay and bluff and drop.
2. Correct help-and-recover or denial techniques.
3. Aggressiveness in the two-on-one-rebounding part of the drill.

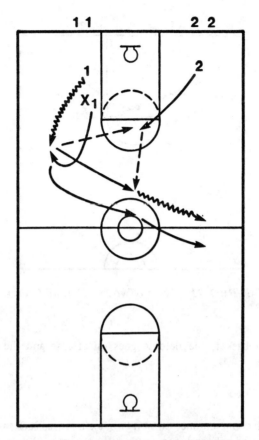

FIGURE 7-20 Two-on-One Drill—Full Court

Drill 48 Two-on-Two Switch (Full Court)

1. The drill begins with offensive player 1 dribbling toward the middle of the court. Defensive player X1 slides with the dribbler.
2. Offensive player 2 moves in to set a pick for player 1. Defensive player X2 will be playing off and toward the ball. As the pick is being set, player X2 will yell out "switch."
3. Player X1 steps behind the pick and picks up offensive player 2.
4. Player X2 steps up on the backside of the pick or screen and picks up offensive player 1. Player X2 must stay low so that the offensive player cannot move by him. Player X2 should try to force the dribbler to the outside or wide.
5. The picks and switches are run continually down the court until in scoring position.
6. On a missed shot, the drill becomes a two-on-two rebounding drill until a layup is scored or until the defense gains possession.

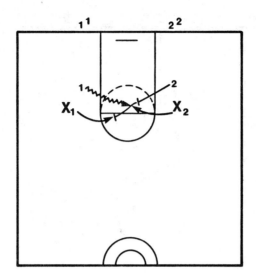

FIGURE 7-21 Two-on-Two Switch (Full Court)

7. After a basket, the defense goes on offense and the offense goes on defense.

Teaching Points

1. Defensive one-on-one, two-on-two techniques, such as forcing to the outside and help and recover.
2. Dribbling, passing, picks, and screens.
3. Switching techniques.
4. Aggressiveness on the rebounding and layup drill.

Drill 49 Two-on-Two—Double Team (Full Court)—Same Positions as in Drill 48

1. Defensive player 1 assumes good defensive position with the head and eyes on the ball and knees bent. Player 2 is in the help-and-recover position.
2. Player X1 plays aggressive defense on player 1. He tries to force player 1 into turning his back as he dribbles or tries to force him toward player 2.
3. If player 1 turns his back, player X2 goes immediately to the ball looking for the steal.
4. If player 1 dribbles toward player X2, player X2 yells out "double," or another signal, and races to player 1 to force him to pick up the ball. Player X2 should extend both arms upward to prevent reaching for a foul.

5. As the double team begins, player X1 looks to bother the ball with both arms extended straight out from the chest. If player 1 cannot pass to player 2, he or she will usually reverse-pivot and look to pass. This move brings the ball directly into the defensive man.
6. If the defense gets the ball, they try to score. If player 1 gets the ball to player 2, player X2 picks up player 2, player X1 moves to a helping position, and the drill continues. If the offense gets the ball down court, they attempt to score. After the score, players switch from offense to defense and from defense to offense.

Teaching Points

1. Defensive stance and positioning.
2. Communication between defensive players.
3. Recovery if the double team does not prove to be successful.
4. Correct timing of the move to double team.

Drill 50 Two on Two—Angle or Jump Switch
(Full Court)—Same Positions as in Drill 48

1. Defensive player X1, who is in good defensive position, slides with the dribbler toward the middle of the court.
2. As the dribbler moves toward player X2, player X2 yells "jump" and moves immediately toward offensive player 1 as if there were a double team coming. Player 2 must be very aggressive and intent on forcing the offensive player to pick up the ball and look to pass to player 2.
3. As player X2 jumps to stop the dribble, player X1 cuts close to the back of teammate X2, directly on a line between players 1 and 2, looking to make a steal of the pass from player 1 to player 2.
4. If player 1 gets the ball to player 2, the defense adjusts and attempts another jump switch.
5. The drill continues to the end basket, where the offense attempts to score. If a shot is missed, the players continue with a two-on-two rebounding drill until someone scores.
6. After a score, the defense moves to offense, the offense moves to defense, and the drill continues to the other end of the court.

Teaching Points

1. Emphasize defensive stance.
2. Knowledge of floor positioning should be emphasized, stressing the relationship of the player and the ball.
3. Stress communication between defensive players.
4. Aggressiveness on defense and rebounding should also be stressed.

FULL COURT DRILLS

Drill 51 Pressure on the Ball—Defending
the Screen Away (Full Court)

1. Player 1 has possession of the ball while standing out-of-bounds.
2. Player 2 screens away from the ball in order to free player 3 for a pass from player 1.
3. Player X1 plays on the strong hand of player 1, with the hands up and moving. If the pass comes in to either player 2 or 3, player X2 stays with player 1.
4. Players X2 and X3 can stay with their assigned man or switch as the screen is being made.
5. If the ball comes in successfully, the drill continues over the full court in a three-on-three situation. The offense uses picks, give-and-go moves, and so forth.
6. At the other end, the offense goes on defense and the defense moves to offense. After running the drill both ways, the next six players jump in.

Teaching Points

1. All aspects of one-on-one defense should be stressed.
2. Stress staying with your own man or switching.
3. There must be communication between players: they must talk when on defense.

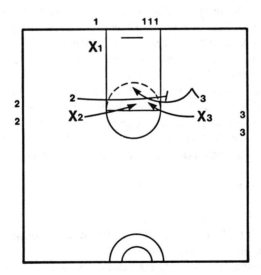

FIGURE 7-22 Pressure on the Ball—Defending the Screen Away (Full Court)

4. These moves teach the beginnings of full court man-for-man pressing defense or the zone press fundamentals.

Drill 52 Pressure on Ball—Defending the Movements from the Stack (Full Court)

1. Players 2 and 3 move into stack positions facing the ball, while teammate 1 has the ball out-of-bounds.
2. Player X2 plays in front of the stack with his back to the ball, watching the moves of players 2 and 3. Player X2 covers the first cutter.
3. Player X3 plays behind the stack facing the ball or between player 3 and the ball. Player X3 takes the second cutter.
4. Player X1 plays on the strong hand of player 1, who is throwing the ball in-bounds. Player X1 stays with player 1 if the ball comes in.
5. With the ball in-bounds, the drill continues as a three-on-three game to the other end of the court.
6. If the defense steals the ball, they should try to score.

Teaching Points

1. Emphasize extreme pressure on not letting the ball in. Remind the defenders to play strong defense for only five seconds, because there will be a violation by the offense if the ball is not passed in-bounds before that time.

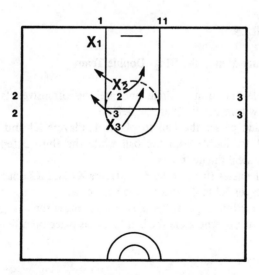

FIGURE 7-23 Pressure on the Ball—Defending Movements from the Stack (Full Court)

2. Stress communication.
3. Players should make the transition quickly to offense if there is a steal.

Drill 53   No Pressure on the Ball—Look for a Double Team on the First Pass Receiver—Same Positions as in Drill 52

1. Player X1 plays in the foul lane facing the stack, rather than pressuring the ball which is in possession of player 1, who is out-of-bounds.
2. Players X2 and X3 play on each side of the stack and are ready to deny a pass to either player 2 or 3.
3. If the ball comes in successfully, player X1 immediately goes to the ball in order to double-team with player X3.
4. If player 1 gets the ball back from player 3, players X1 and X2 move to double-team the new ball handler.
5. After the ball penetrates past the free-throw line, the drill continues down court in a three-on-three game.

Teaching Points

1. Stress communication. The players should know where the ball is.
2. Emphasize basic one-on-one defense.
3. Correct double-teaming methods should be emphasized so that the ball handler cannot split or make a successful pass.
4. Stress aggressiveness and hustle.

VARIATION DRILLS

Drill 54   Three Men in the Ring—Double Team

1. Eight players form a circle and are the offensive players. The three players within the circle are on defense.
2. The coach passes the ball to player 1. Players X1 and X2 immediately attempt to double-team the ball while the third defensive player, X3, looks to steal the next pass.
3. Player 1 passes successfully and players X1 and X2 double-team the ball, while player X2 looks to steal the next pass.
4. If a pass is intercepted, the player who threw the pass goes into the ring and the player who stole the ball takes his place on offense.

Teaching Points

1. Stress footwork and body balance.

2. The players should know where the ball is and be ready to double-team and intercept.
3. Emphasize aggressiveness.

Drill 55   Zone Defense Drill

1. Player X1 is positioned at what would be considered a zone wing position. Players 1, 3, 4, and 5 take positions around player X1.
2. The ball is passed quickly from one offensive player to the other. Player X1 must shift his position quickly as the ball is passed and moves to a position between the offensive players and the basket when the ball is passed to players 1, 3, and 4.
3. When the ball is passed to player 5 in the pivot position, player X1 drops back toward player 5 so as to jam or crowd his movement.

Teaching Points

1. Quick reactions by player X1 as the ball is passed.
2. Overhead passes by the offense.
3. Player X1 should move his hands in the passing lanes.

Drill 56   Three-on-Two Drill—Tandem Movements

1. Player X1 starts the drill at the free-throw line, in good defensive position.
2. Player X2 is in the free-throw lane, directly behind player X1. Players 1, 2, and 3 are on offense. Dribbling is allowed only toward the basket.

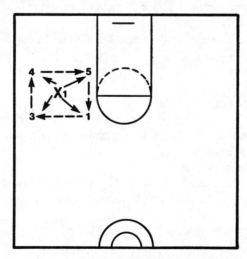

FIGURE 7-24   Zone Defense Drill

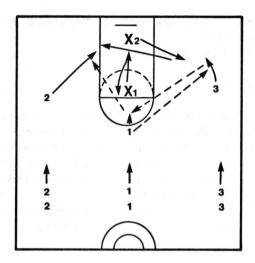

FIGURE 7-25 Three-on-Two Drill—Tandem Movements

3. Player X2 is to cover the first pass. Example: player 1 passes to player 3; player X2 moves to cover player 3 while player X1 drops back to the area vacated by player X2.
4. As player X2 gets good positioning on player 3 to try to force him to the outside, player X1 plays the three-second lane in such a way that he faces player 1 in an angle between the ball and player 2.
5. If the ball is returned to player 1, player X1 races out to challenge the ball and player X2 drops back into the lane.
6. As the ball comes to player 2, player X2 moves out to challenge the ball and player X1 drops back.
7. The defense must stop three series, and then the players rotate positions.

Teaching Points

1. Stress good defensive balance.
2. Footwork—racing up to challenge the ball; backward movement and lateral movement—should be stressed. The back man should react and cover the first pass.
3. Emphasize weak-side help.
4. Aggressiveness and hustle should be stressed. Players should force a jump shot and not allow a layup when they are outnumbered by the offense.

Drill 57 Loose-Ball Recovery Drill (Full Court)

1. The coach or a designated person stands on the side of the court. The players are numbered 1, 2, 3, 4, and form four lines at the baseline facing

into the court. A signal is called out by the coach as the ball is rolled toward the free-throw area.
2. For example, if "odd" is called, then players 1 and 3 race for the ball. When the player retrieves the ball, he yells out "ball" and turns to face the basket.
3. The other player must take a defensive position immediately and attempt to make the offensive player dribble toward the sideline or force him or her to pick up the ball.
4. The players stay in this one-on-one drill until someone scores. For example, player 1 grabs the ball and tries to score against the defense of player 3. Player 3 steals the ball or rebounds a shot, and in turn player 3 attempts to score against player 1.

Teaching Points

1. Alertness and aggressiveness when reacting to the ball—players should always know where the ball is.
2. Stress communication—yelling out "ball" to teammates.
3. Emphasize defensive work.
4. Emphasize dribbling and shooting.
5. Stress rebounding.

8

Combination Drills

INTRODUCTION

The term combination means that more than one fundamental basketball technique is employed in a particular drill. It will be difficult to incorporate many combination drills into the instruction given to beginning players until such time as they have been able to master or at least become relatively efficient when executing each fundamental separately.

As players advance in their ability to execute individual techniques, we recommend that coaches begin to introduce combination drills into practice sessions. This strategy will help save valuable instructional or practice time, but, more importantly, it will allow the players to participate in situations that are more game-like and will give them an understanding that they should work to become complete players.

The following drills vary in that some emphasize passing, dribbling, and shooting skills, while others place greater emphasis on offensive and defensive reactions as well as rebounding. This is not an all-inclusive listing of combination drills and should encourage coaches to create drills that may correspond more closely to the team offense or defense method that they will be teaching. Once players have reached a certain level of accomplishment, the coach should plan drills that meet his team's needs and try to combine the teaching of fundamentals with team movements and responsibilities.

DRILLS THAT INCLUDE OFFENSE AND DEFENSE

Drill 1   Dribble, Pivot, Pass (Handoff)

1. Offensive players 1 and 2 are at the sideline, and defensive players 3 and 4 are at two designated spots on the court. This drill is run from sideline to sideline, allowing more than one group to work at the same time.
2. Player 1 dribbles toward the first defensive player who forces player 1 to move to his right. Player 1 stops, pivots, and hands off to player 2, who is a trailer.
3. After player 2 receives the ball, he dribbles toward the next defensive player, stops, pivots, and passes to player 1, who trails behind him.
4. Player 1 stops on the sideline, pivots, and throws a baseball pass to the first defensive player, player 3, who has moved to a position at the opposite sideline.
5. The two defensive players move to offense, while players 1 and 2 become the defensive players.

Teaching Points

1. Use of the protection dribble when approaching the defensive player.
2. Correct reverse pivot and handoff by the dribbler.
3. Timing on the cut by the player receiving the handoff.
4. Proper bluff-and-drop procedure by the defensive player.

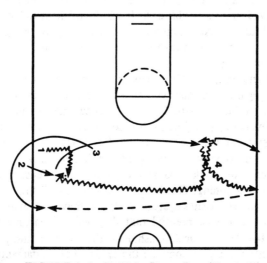

FIGURE 8-1   Dribble, Pivot, Pass (Handoff)

Drill 2 Dribbling, Passing Drill

1. The players are divided into three lines as indicated. The drill begins with player 1 in possession of the ball.
2. Player 1 dribbles through the chairs and drives to the basket for a layup. Player 1 recovers the rebound and passes to player 2 at the outlet position. Player 1 then goes to the end of line 2.
3. Player 2 receives the pass from player 1 and throws a long pass to player 3 (baseball; two-handed). Player 2 then cuts hard toward the foul line ready to receive a bounce pass (or chest pass) from player 3. After receiving this pass, player 2 shoots a jump shot and then goes to the end of line 3.
4. Player 3, after passing to player 2, moves to the end of line 4.
5. Two players from line 4 set up in the lane and attempt to rebound the shot by player 2. Player 4, who gains possession of the rebound, uses a

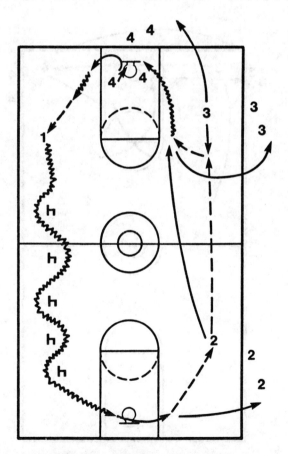

FIGURE 8-2 *Dribbling, Passing Drill*

blast-out dribble and moves to a position where he can dribble through the chairs, following the pattern set by player 1.

6. A new player from line 4 joins the player who did not obtain the rebound, and they prepare to rebound the next shot. Thus the only chance to get into the dribbling and shooting action is to gain possession of a rebound.

Teaching Point

1. Stress techniques of passing, dribbling, shooting, and rebounding.

Drill 3 Four Corners

1. Line 1 is the shooting line, line 2 is the rebounder, line 3 is the passer, and line 4 is the feeder.
2. Line 3 passes to line 4, as line 2 fakes and cuts to the free-throw lane.

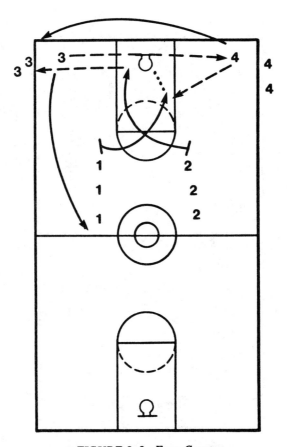

FIGURE 8-3 Four Corners

3. Line 1 fakes and cuts off line 2 and is fed a pass by line 4. Line 1 shoots a layup shot or a jump shot. (A variation is to have line 4 dribble to the free-throw lane and screen for line 1.)
4. Line 2 rebounds and passes to line 3, and the next four players continue the drill.
5. All players rotate to the next line to their right.

Teaching Points

1. Stress techniques of faking and cutting without the ball, passing, shooting, and rebounding.
2. Emphasize the continuous movement of all players.
   Dribbling and Shooting, Passing and Dribbling Drills

DRIBBLING AND SHOOTING, PASSING AND DRIBBLING DRILLS

Drill 4 Dribble-Drive and Shoot—Change of Direction—Dribble from the Corners

1. Each player (or as many players as possible) has possession of a ball.
2. Player 2 dribbles toward the right corner. When he reaches the corner, he uses a reverse (or crossover) dribble and drives to the basket for a lay-up shot. Player 2 recovers his own ball and dribbles to line 1 on the inside of the court.
3. As player 2 reaches the corner, player 1 dribbles toward the left corner,

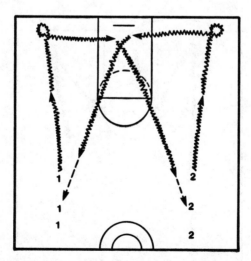

FIGURE 8-4 *Dribble-Drive and Shoot—Change of Direction—Dribble from the Corners*

reverse-dribbles, and drives. The players must time their drives so that they do not collide on the layup shot attempt. Player 2 goes to line 1 and player 1 goes to line 2.

Teaching Points

1. Using correct change-of-direction dribble technique.
2. Adjusting the layup shot release according to the angle of the drive to the basket.

Drill 5   Dribble-Drive, Reverse-Dribble, and Shoot the Layup

1. Same procedure as in Drill 4.
2. The players use a reverse dribble from the corner, move to the edge of the foul line, use another reverse dribble, and drive to the basket.
3. The players recover the ball and move to the opposite line.

Teaching Points

1. Correct change-of-direction technique.
2. Strong drive to the basket.
3. Use of left and right hands.

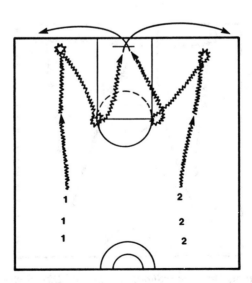

FIGURE 8-5   *Dribble-Drive, Reverse-Dribble, and Shoot the Layup*

Drill 6 Dribble-Drive and Shoot the Jump Shot

1. Same procedure as in Drill 5.
2. The players shoot a jump shot after making their second reverse dribble at the edge of the foul line.

Teaching Points

1. Stop on-balance.
2. Shoot quickly.

Drill 7 One on One from the Key
Using Three-Line Passing Drill

1. The players are positioned in three lines as indicated.
2. Player 1 dribbles toward the circle, crosses over to the right, and makes a pass to player 2, who fakes and steps toward the pass. After making the pass, player 1 cuts to the basket looking for a return pass and stops at a position near the foul lane block, if he does not receive the pass from player 2.
3. As the pass is made from player 1 to player 2, player 3 fakes toward the basket, cuts toward the foul lane to receive a pass from player 2, and prepares to make a handoff to player 2.
4. Player 2 passes to player 3 and then cuts to the foul-line area to receive a handoff pass from player 3. When player 2 receives the pass from player 3, he or she is ready to play a one-on-one game with player 3.

FIGURE 8–6 *One on One from the Key Using Three-Line Passing Drill*

5. Player 1 is ready to be a defensive helper for player 3 and may step in player 2's path and force him or her to shoot a jump shot. Player 1 may also be told not to get involved in the play at all.
6. Player 1 goes to line 3, player 2 goes to line 1, and player 3 goes to line 2.

Teaching Points

1. Good passes—timing the pass and cutting toward the ball.
2. Movement to receive the ball.
3. Quick adjustment to the defense.

ONE-ON-ONE DRILLS

Drill 8 One on One from the Side—Using Three-Man Passing Drill

1. Same positions as in Drill 7.
2. Player 1 passes to player 2, cuts to the outside of him, and takes a position near the offensive corner.
3. As the pass is made from player 1 to player 2, player 3 fakes and cuts to the foul lane to receive a pass from player 2. Player 2 then cuts to the outside of line 2 and moves to the block on the weak side to be ready to help with weak-side defense and rebounding.
4. Player 3 passes to player 1 and moves quickly to defend against player 1 in a one-on-one game from the corner.
5. Players rotate lines.

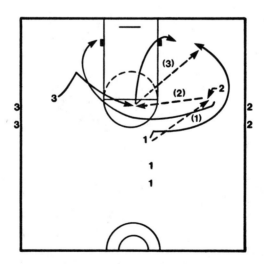

FIGURE 8-7 *One on One from the Side—Using Three-Man Passing Drill*

Teaching Points

1. Fundamentals of good passing.
2. Movement to receive the ball.
3. Quick adjustment to defense.
4. An understanding that weak-side help is important.

Drill 9 One on One–Defense Practice in Going "Over the Top" of a Screen

1. Same positions as in Drill 8.
2. Player 1 passes to player 2, cuts to the basket, and positions himself at the block. Player 1 then moves back up the lane to become a screener for player 2.
3. Player 3 cuts and receives a pass from player 2 at the foul-line area. After player 2 passes to player 3, player 2 cuts to the foul-line area to receive a handoff from player 3 and begin a one-on-one game.
4. Player 2 tries to drive defensive player 3 into the screen near player 1. Player 3 fights over the top and does not go behind the screen. Player 1 should talk and warn teammate, player 3, about the screen.

Teaching Points

1. Fundamentals of good passing.
2. Movement to receive the ball.
3. Good techniques after reaction to defense.
4. Correct method of driving defensive player into a screen.

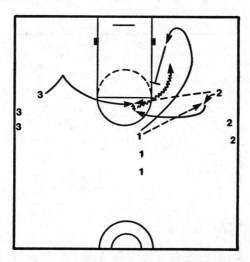

FIGURE 8-8 *One on One–Defense Practice in Going "Over the Top" of a Screen*

5. Fighting over the top of the screen.
6. Talking on defense.

TWO-ON-TWO DRILLS

Drill 10 Two on Two, Help and Recover
from the Three-Line Passing Drill

1. Player 1 passes to player 2 and cuts outside to a position in the corner. After player 2 reaches the corner position, player 4 moves into a position that is between player 1 and the foul line.
2. Player 3 cuts to the foul line for a pass from player 2. Player 2 cuts immediately behind player 3 to receive a handoff from player 3. Players 2 and 3 play a one-on-one game, and player 3 forces player 2 to drive to the right.
3. Player 4 moves to stop player 2's drive. When player 2 is forced to stop by player 4, he passes quickly to player 1. Player 4 must now recover quickly from the help position to prevent player 1 from driving to the basket or from taking an easy jump shot.
4. Player 1 goes to line 4, player 4 goes to line 3, player 3 goes to line 2, and player 2 goes to line 1.
5. Emphasis should be placed on techniques stressed in Drills 8 and 9.

Teaching Point

1. Help-and-recovery technique.

FIGURE 8-9 Two on Two, Help and Recover from the Three-Line Passing Drill

**Drill 11 Three-Line Passing—Two on Two,
Beat the Man to the Spot, and Take
Away the Weak-Side Cut**

1. Player 1 passes to player 2 and cuts outside of him to a position in the corner.
2. Player 3 cuts to the foul-line area to receive a pass from player 2. After passing to player 3, player 2 cuts around player 3 to the weak-side block position.
3. Player 4 moves to a position in the lane as player 2 makes the pass to player 3. Player 4 will try to deny player 2's cut toward the ball after it is passed to player 1 in the corner.
4. Player 3 passes to player 1 and moves to defend against him. As player 1 receives the pass from player 3, he looks inside and tries to pass to player 2, who cuts from the weak side toward the ball.
5. Player 1 goes to line 4, player 4 goes to line 3, player 3 goes to line 2, and player 2 goes to line 1.

Teaching Points

1. Emphasis should be placed on the techniques stressed in Drills 7 through 10.
2. The correct techniques for the offensive player making the weak-side cut and the defensive player denying the weak-side cut should also be stressed.

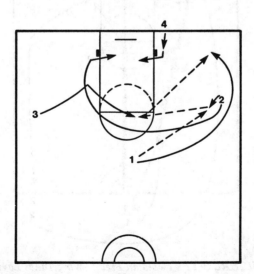

FIGURE 8-10 *Three-Line Passing—Two on Two, Beat the Man to the Spot, and Take Away the Weak-Side Cut.*

Drill 12   Two-Man Break—Wing Takes Layup

1. The players are positioned in two lines at midcourt, as indicated.
2. Player 1 dribbles hard and fast to the free-throw line, fakes a pass to the opposite side, then passes to player 2.
3. Player 2 runs parallel to the dribbler and at the free-throw-line extended area, he cuts to the basket, receives the pass, and takes a layup shot.
4. After the shot, player 2 moves to receive an outlet pass on the opposite side of the lane.
5. Player 1 follows player 2's shot, steps out-of-bounds, and makes an outlet pass to player 2, who takes three or four dribbles and passes to the next player in line 1.
6. Player 2 goes to line 1 and player 1 goes to line 2.

Teaching Points

1. Stress the fundamentals of dribbling, passing, and faking.
2. The cutter must be even with the ball handler (dribbler).
3. Emphasize following shots.
4. Stress playing a transition game with the in-bounds pass.

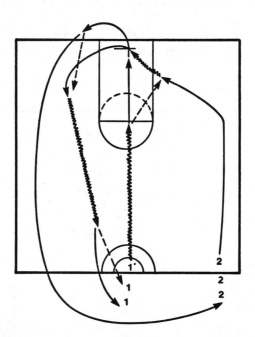

FIGURE 8-11   *Two-Man Break—Wing Takes Layup*

Drill 13 Wing Man Dribbles and Drives for a Layup

1. Player 1 passes to player 2 and moves to a position toward the basket that will allow him to bother the shooter.
2. Player 2 dribbles hard to the free-throw-line extended area, uses a crossover dribble, goes toward the basket, fakes a pass, and goes for a layup.
3. Player 1 rebounds and makes an outlet pass to player 2, who moves to a position on the opposite side of the floor. Player 2 takes three or four dribbles and makes a pass to the next player at midcourt.
4. Player 1 goes to line 2 and player 2 goes to line 1.

Teaching Points

1. Stress crossover dribbling.
2. Approaching for the shot, player 2 should concentrate on making the fake with the eyes and head.
3. Players should make strong power-layup shots.
4. Stress the beginning of the transition game with the in-bounds pass.

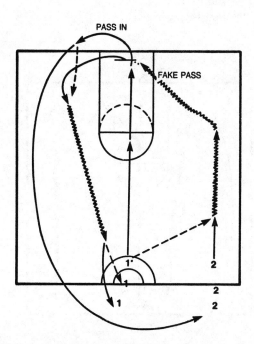

FIGURE 8-12 Wing Man Dribbles and Drives for a Layup

Drill 14 Wing Man Dribbles,
Fakes, and Passes to Middle

1. Player 1 passes to player 2 on the wing and cuts to the free-throw-line area.
2. Player 2 dribbles hard to the free-throw-line extended area, changes direction, and drives hard toward the basket. Player 2 makes a quick stop near the block at the side of the lane.
3. As player 2 makes his stop, player 1 breaks to the basket ready to receive a pass for the layup.
4. Player 1 continues through to the outlet area on the opposite side after taking the shot.
5. Player 2 rebounds and makes the outlet to player 1, who takes three or four dribbles before giving a pass to the next player at the beginning of line 1.
6. Player 1 goes to line 2, and player 2 goes to line 1 as the drill continues.

Teaching Points

1. Dribbling, passing, and making an on-balance stop.
2. Shooting properly while on the move.
3. Following the shot.
4. Beginning the transition game.

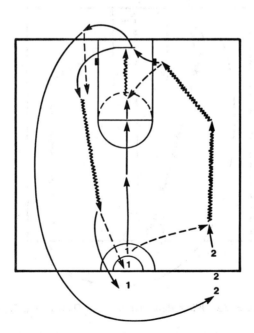

FIGURE 8-13 *Wing Man Dribbles, Drives, Fakes, and Passes to Middle*

**Drill 15 Wing Dribbles, Passes to
Middle Man for Jump Shot**

1. Player 1 dribbles two or three times, makes a chest pass to player 2, and continues to the free-throw line.
2. Player 2 dribbles down the sideline, fakes a drive to the basket, and gives a pass to player 1, who takes a jump shot.
3. If there is a rebound, player 2 retrieves it and gives a quick outlet pass to player 1.
4. The drill is completed as in Drill 14.

Teaching Points

1. Dribbling, passing, and keeping lanes wide.
2. Being ready to receive a pass in shooting position—the receiver's hands and feet should be positioned in such a manner that he or she may take a quick shot.
3. Using jump shot skills.
4. Rebounding correctly.

Drill 16 Tip-In of a Missed Layup

1. Player 1 dribbles hard and fast to the free-throw line and comes to a stop. He fakes to the opposite side and gives a pass to player 2.

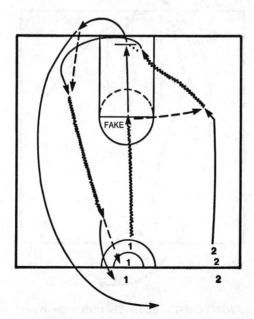

FIGURE 8-14 Tip-In of a Missed Layup

2. Player 2 drives in for the layup, but this time player 2 places the ball off the goal or the backboard. Player 1 follows from the free-throw line, ready to tap in the missed shot.

3. Player 2 goes to the outlet area on the opposite side. Player 1 rebounds and makes an in-bounds pass to player 2.

Teaching Points

1. Dribbling and passing.
2. Good head-and-eye fakes by the passer.
3. Stopping at the free-throw line.
4. Timing the jump for the missed shot and tipping with the finger tips.
5. Following the shot.

THREE-MAN DRILLS

Drill 17   Jump Shot from the Wing

1. With a defensive player positioned in the three-second lane, player 1 dribbles toward the basket and forces the defense to play him.
2. Player 1 makes a pass to player 2. It is now a two-on-one situation from which player 2 may go for the layup or take a jump shot.

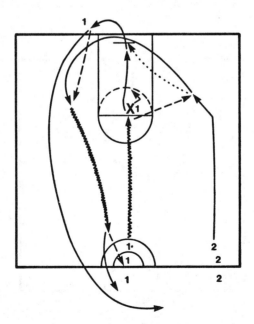

FIGURE 8-15   Jump Shot from the Wing

3. The defensive player bluffs toward the offensive player and either re-bounds or gains possession after the made basket. On a rebound, the defensive player makes the outlet pass to player 2. When a basket is scored, the defensive player steps out-of-bounds and makes a quick in-bounds pass to player 2.

4. Player 1 moves to the defense, player 2 goes to line 1, and the defensive player (X1) goes to line 1.

Teaching Points

1. Dribbling and passing.
2. Stopping at the free-throw-line in control and faking.
3. Defensive and offensive fundamentals in a two-on-one situation. The offense must force the defensive player to commit himself by using fakes and quick ball movement. The defense must use bluffing and faking tactics in order to force the offensive player to shoot a jump shot rather than a layup.

**Drill 18 Two on Two from
Three-Line Passing Drill**

1. Player 1 passes to player 2 and cuts toward the basket looking for a re-turn pass. Player 1 cuts to the block and then returns to a position along the side of the lane to set a screen for player 2.

2. Player 3 cuts to the foul lane and receives a pass from player 2, who cuts immediately behind player 3 to receive a handoff from him. Player 4

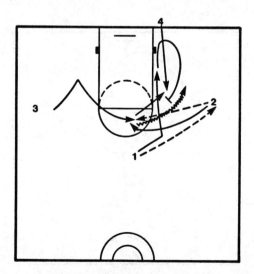

FIGURE 8-16 Two-on-Two from Three-Line Passing Drill

moves from the baseline position to defend against the screener, player 1.
3. Player 2 tries to drive player 3 into the screen being set by player 1.
4. The defense may work on the slide-through, hedge, switch, or double-team.
5. Player 1 goes to line 4, player 4 goes to line 3, player 3 goes to line 2, and player 2 goes to line 1.

Teaching Points

1. Correct passing technique.
2. Movement to receive the ball.
3. Quick adjustment by the defense—talking and helping; and especially, using the correct procedure for guarding the player setting the screen.

Drill 19   Give and Go—Pass, Cut, and Replace—No Dribble

1. Players are positioned in three lines as indicated.
2. Player 1 passes to player 2, fakes away, and cuts to the basket. If player 1 does not receive the pass from player 2, he or she moves toward the wing position to replace player 3, after stopping at the deep-block position.
3. Player 3 cuts to the foul line to replace player 1. Player 3 receives the pass from player 2 and turns to face the basket.

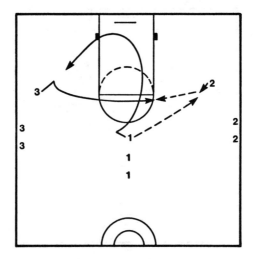

FIGURE 8-17   Give and Go—Pass, Cut, and Replace—No Dribble

**Drill 20 Give and Go—Pass, Cut,
and Replace Continuation**

4. Player 3 passes to player 1 and cuts to the basket looking for the return
   pass from him. If player 3 does not receive the pass, he or she moves to the
   deep-block position and then out to the wing position to replace player 2.
5. Player 1 passes to player 2 at the foul-line area. Player 2 turns to face the
   basket and is ready to pass quickly to player 3.
6. Player 1 goes to line 2, player 2 goes to line 3, and player 3 goes to line 1.

Teaching Points

1. Stress cutting moves using change of pace and faking, and correct hand
   position by the cutter as he moves toward the basket.
2. Emphasize movement to receive the ball and correct hand position of the
   player who is receiving the pass.
3. Stress quick passing and cutting by players to replace each other.
4. The player who receives the pass should turn to face the basket in a
   triple-threat position.
5. Continue the drill for as many times as necessary.

**Drill 21 Give and Go—Change of Direction
on an Overplay by the Defense**

1. Players are positioned in three lines as indicated.
2. Player 1 passes to player 2 and cuts to the basket, looking for a return

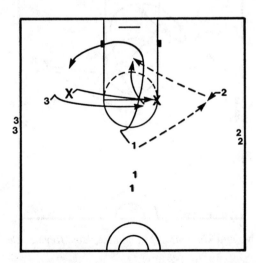

FIGURE 8-18 Give and Go—Change of Direction on an Overplay by the Defense

pass from him. If player 1 does not receive the pass, player 1 moves to the deep-block position and then toward the wing to replace player 3.
3. Player 3 cuts toward the circle and toward player 2. Player 2 fakes the pass to player 3 in this situation because the defensive player (X) is over-playing player 3 and denying a pass from player 2.
4. Player 2 passes to player 3, who makes a cut to the basket behind the defensive player.

Teaching Points

1. Stress a quick change of direction and cut to the basket by the player being overplayed.
2. The coach may take the position of the defensive player so that he may show player 3 exactly how to make the reverse cut when being overplayed.

Drill 22 Give and Go—Pass, Cut, and Replace; Reverse Cut and Pass Off the Dribble

1. Players are positioned in three lines as indicated.
2. Player 1 passes to player 2 and then fakes and cuts to the basket. If player 1 does not receive the pass from player 2, player 1 moves toward the wing position to replace player 3.
3. Player 3 cuts toward the foul-line area, timing the cut so that he or she moves just as player 1 makes his cut. Player 2 passes to player 3 near the top of the foul circle. Player 3 turns and starts a drive toward the basket.

FIGURE 8-19 Give and Go—Pass, Cut, and Replace; Reverse Cut and Pass Off the Dribble

4. As player 3 drives toward the basket, player 3 stops and makes a bounce pass to player 1, who makes a quick cut to the basket. Player 1 makes the cut to the basket after a signal by player 3 or just as player 3 stops dribble. An example of a signal for this cut could be eye contact between players 3 and 1.
5. Player 1 goes to line 2, player 2 goes to line 3, and player 3 goes to line 1.

Teaching Points

1. Proper timing of cuts to the basket and toward the ball.
2. Using correct form when making the bounce pass.

Drill 23   Give and Go—Pass and Cut Off a Backscreen—Pass from the Dribbling Position

1. Players are positioned as indicated.
2. Player 1 passes to player 2 and cuts away from the direction of his pass. As player 1 passes to player 2, player 3 cuts toward the edge of the foul circle and sets a backscreen for player 1.
3. After receiving the pass from player 1, player 2 starts a drive toward the foul line and makes a quick pass to player 1, who has cut off the screen by player 3.
4. Player 1 goes to line 2, player 2 goes to line 3, and player 3 goes to line 1.

FIGURE 8-20 Give and Go—Pass and Cut Off a Backscreen—Pass from the Dribbling Position

Teaching Points

1. Proper backscreen by player 3.
2. Use of the left-hand dribble by player 2—he or she should use the outside hand or the hand away from the defense.
3. Correct timing and execution of the one-hand push pass by player 2.

Drill 24 Give and Go—Pass and Cut Off
a Backscreen—Pass Off the Dribble

1. Players are positioned as indicated.
2. Player 1 passes to player 2, fakes, and cuts to the basket looking for a return pass from player 2. If he does not receive the pass, player 1 starts to the wing position as if to replace player 3.
3. Player 3 fakes toward the middle and then reverses toward the basket. He cuts off a backscreen by player 1 and looks to receive a pass from player 2.
4. Player 2 drives toward the foul line and makes a quick pass to player 3.
5. After screening, player 1 steps toward player 2 ready to receive a pass if player 2 does not make the pass to player 3.
6. Player 1 goes to line 2, player 2 goes to line 3, and player 3 goes to line 1.

Teaching Points

1. Proper backscreen.
2. Correct cut to the basket and off the screen.
3. Correct timing between the cutter and passer.

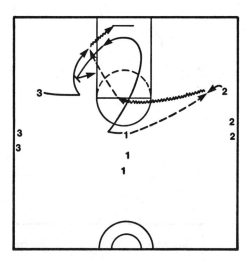

FIGURE 8-21   Give and Go—Pass and Cut Off a Backscreen—Pass Off the Dribble

Drill 25 Give and Go—Pass, Screen
Away, and Pass to the Screener

1. Player 1 passes to player 2 and screens away for player 3.
2. Player 3 fakes and cuts off the screen by player 1, looking for a pass from player 2.
3. Player 1 moves toward the ball after setting the screen for player 3.
4. Player 2 may pass to either player 3 or 1, who may take either a driving layup or a jump shot.
5. Player 1 goes to line 2, player 2 goes to line 3, and player 3 goes to line 1.

Teaching Points

1. Movement after passing.
2. Proper screen away from the ball by player 1 and then cutting quickly back toward the ball.

TEAM DRILLS

Drill 26 Single Defender Against
Four Offensive Players

1. Players are positioned as indicated, with player X3 the lone defender.
2. Player 1 starts the drill after a signal from the coach. He tries to pass to player 3, but player X3 denies the pass to player 3. Player 1 then passes to player 2.

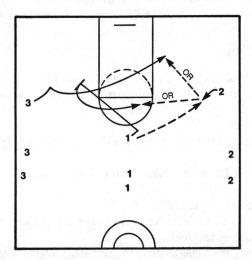

FIGURE 8-22 Give and Go—Pass, Screen Away, and Pass to the Screener

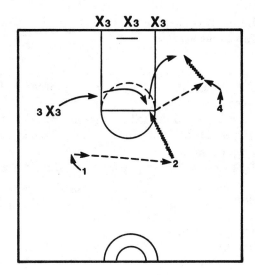

FIGURE 8-23 *Single Defender Against Four Offensive Players*

3. As the pass is made from player 1 to player 2, player X3 moves to a position on the edge of the foul lane so that he will be in a helping position on the weak side.
4. After player 2 receives the pass from player 1, he drives hard to the basket. Player X3 moves quickly to prevent player 2's drive and forces him to stop the dribble.
5. When player 2 is forced to stop, player 4 moves quickly into a position to receive a pass and make a baseline drive. Player X3 moves quickly to a position where he can take the charge or force player 4 to stop his drive.

Teaching Points

1. Good denial defense moves on passes to the wing.
2. Opening up to the ball as the pass is made away from the player being defended.
3. Footwork.
4. Help for the defense coming from the weak side to help on the ball.

Drill 27   Single Defender Against Four Offensive Players

1. Same positioning as in Drill 26.
2. In this situation, player X3 allows the pass to player 3 and moves to play one on one against him.
3. If player 3 is unable to drive to the basket, player 3 returns the pass to

FIGURE 8-24   *Single Defender Against Four Offensive Players*

player 1, and player X3 drops off to a helping position. Player X3 drops off even more as player 1 passes to player 2.

4. Stress same movements as in previous drill.
5. Stress same fundamentals as in Drill 26.

Drill 28   Deny a Cut Toward the Ball, Front a Post Player, Weak-Side Helping Position

1. The players are positioned in a line as indicated. The first player in the line moves to a defensive position against the first player in line, who has possession of the ball.
2. 1 passes to the coach or manager, C1, and cuts to the basket. X1 moves to a position (A) that will force 1 to cut behind him. After player 1 reaches a position deep in the lane (under the basket), he or she makes a hard cut toward C1 looking to receive a pass from the coach. X1 denies 1's cut to the ball and prevents the pass from the coach (B).
3. When 1 does not receive the pass from C1 by the time he or she reaches the foul line position, 1 pivots and moves down the lane looking for a pass from C2 (who has received a pass from C1). X1 fronts player 1, as the offensive player makes his cut (C) down the lane, and prevents the pass from C2. If 1 does not receive the pass from C2, he moves across the lane to the weak side, and X1 moves to the weak side help position (D). X1 is ready to react to a drive made by the coach.
4. X1 moves to the end of the line and offensive player 1 moves to the defensive position against the next player in line 1.

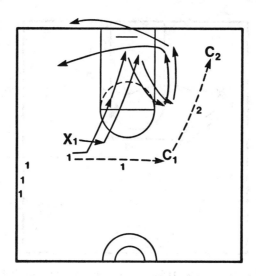

FIGURE 8-25 *Deny a Cut Toward the Ball, Front a Post Player, Weak-Side Helping Position*

Teaching Points

1. Quick defensive moves to deny and overplay the cuts by the offensive player.
2. Proper hand position so that the passing lanes are blocked.
3. Correct foot position and shuffle movement.

9

Transition Drills

INTRODUCTION

An important consideration for coaches is teaching players to make an immediate transition from defense to offense or vice versa. A team that is able to react immediately every time possession of the ball changes will have a tremendous advantage over its opposition.

One advantage of making a quick change from defense to offense is that it will nullify, if not eliminate, pressure defenses by the opposition and afford the offensive team the opportunity to score quick and easy baskets. When a quick basket cannot be scored, the offensive team that reacts immediately when changing from defense to offense can still put tremendous pressure on the defensive team, forcing defensive mistakes.

A quick transition from offense to defense allows pressing defenses to be more effective than when they are set up slowly. A fast-reacting team will be able to nullify the opposing team's fast break and limit its easy-scoring opportunities. A team that is able to prevent, or minimize, the number of easy baskets scored against it will be able to win many games against equal competition and possibly to win against a superior team.

While players are learning the fundamentals of the game and first practicing competitive drills, the coach should emphasize the importance of the transition from one phase of the game to another.

This chapter includes individual and team drills which require a transition to be made every time the ball changes possession. Although drills in transition are especially important for teams whose coaches favor fast-breaking offenses or pressing defenses, all teams must practice it, since they must be prepared to play against teams that are excellent at executing the change from offense to defense and from defense to offense.

**Drill 1   One-on-One Crosscourt–Teammates
on Sideline are Outlet Receivers
for the Offensive Player**

1. The players are positioned as indicated along the baseline and midcourt lines. Players 1 and X1 play a one-on-one game using the crosscourt baskets. This drill may start with a jump ball or with the ball being rolled on the floor, requiring the two players whose numbers are called to try to recover the ball. (This is indicated by the /1\'s in the diagram.) The player who gains possession becomes the offensive player (1), and the

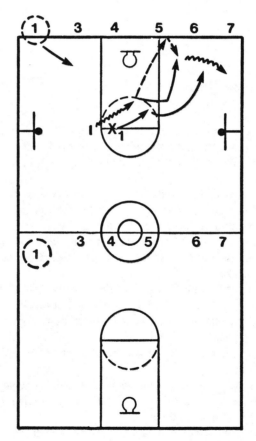

FIGURE 9-1   One-on-One Crosscourt–Teammates on Sideline Are Outlet Receivers for the Offensive Player

other becomes the defensive player (X1). Each line is told which basket it should shoot for before the drill begins.

2. Player 1 tries to drive to the basket. Player X1 must prevent a score, try to recover possession of the ball, and try to score at the opposite basket. Once a player loses possession of the ball, he must react quickly to a defense position and play defense over the full court.

3. The offensive players will have teammates on the sidelines to whom they may pass when they are having difficulty driving past the defensive players. In this diagram, player 1 passes to player 5, makes a fake, and cuts to a position where player 1 may receive a return pass from player 5. The offensive player may pass to any player on either sideline.

4. The coach will determine the number of baskets to be scored by each group. When one pair has completed the drill, the coach calls the next number.

5. Players may be matched according to comparable speed, size, or position.

Teaching Points

1. Stress making a very fast transition from offense to defense and from defense to offense.

2. Players should use teammates as outlets when in trouble and should not try to force the dribble.

3. The defensive player should try to deny a return pass to the offensive player after he or she has made a pass.

Drill 2   One-on-One Full Court—Make Two Baskets

1. The players are positioned in two lines at the end of the court. The first two players in each line are positioned on either side of the basket at the free-throw-lane blocks.

2. The coach shoots a free throw and the ball becomes alive immediately. Players 1 and 2 try to gain possession, whether the shot is made or missed. In this diagram, player 1 gains possession of the ball and tries to dribble up the court in an attempt to score at the far basket. Player 2 moves quickly to prevent a score by player 1.

3. When a score or a recovery is made, the defensive player (2) takes the ball and attempts to score at the other end. Player 1 moves immediately to a defensive position to prevent player 2's penetration.

4. If the defensive player forces the dribbler to stop the dribble without a shot being taken, the offensive player must turn the ball over to the defensive player. The drill will continue in the opposite direction.

5. An alternate to this drill would be to require three baskets to be scored and to allow the player who scores to retain possession of the ball.

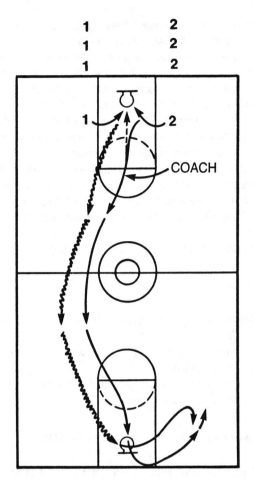

FIGURE 9-2   One-on-One Full Court—Make Two Baskets

Teaching Points

1. Stress making a very fast transition from offense to defense and from defense to offense.
2. Players should use a variety of dribbling techniques to get free.
3. The defensive player should not foul or try to gamble on a steal attempt.

Drill 3   One-on-One Full Court—Make Three
Baskets with Post Man Available

1. The players are positioned in two lines at the baseline.
2. Players 3 and 4 are positioned near midcourt but may move between the

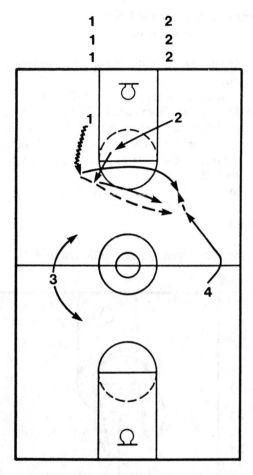

FIGURE 9-3 *One-on-One Full Court—Make Three Baskets with Post Man Available*

time-line hash marks in order to make themselves available as outlet-pass receivers for the offensive player to use when he is in trouble.

3. Players 3 and 4 may only receive and return the pass to offensive player 1. They do not dribble or get involved in the offensive play.
4. The drill responsibilities are the same as in the preceding diagram.

Teaching Points

1. The dribbler should keep the head up, use fakes, not force the action, and use his teammate as an outlet man.
2. The defensive player is to overplay and deny a return pass to player 1.
3. Players should make a very fast change from offense to defense and from defense to offense.

Drill 4   Loose Ball Recovery and Full
Court Drive or Break for the Score

1. Player 1 has possession of the ball in the position near the midcourt line, as indicated.
2. Player X1 defends against player 1's dribble toward the top basket and deflects the ball away from player 1. Player X1 moves quickly to recover the deflected free ball, throws it out in front of him toward midcourt, and races to control the ball and dribble to the basket for a layup.
3. Player 1, who lost possession of the ball, tries to recover and prevent the shot by player X1.
4. Player 1 goes to line X1 and player X1 goes to line 1.

Teaching Points

1. Correct method of making a deflection and steal.

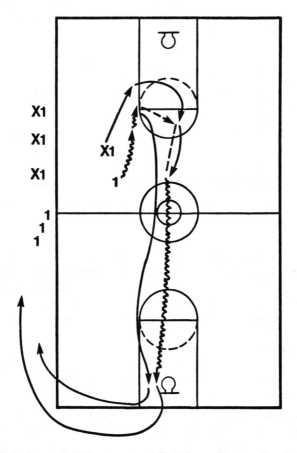

FIGURE 9-4   *Loose Ball Recovery and Full Court Drive or Break for the Score*

2. Quick recovery.
3. Passing the ball out in front and picking it up on the move.
4. Concentration when making the layup.

**Drill 5   Recovery to the Defensive
Position against a Dribbler**

1. Players are positioned in two lines near midcourt.
2. Player 1 starts the drill by passing to player 2, and player 2 drives quickly toward the basket. Player 1 must sprint to get ahead of player 2, gain defensive position, and force the dribbler to change direction or stop.
3. If a shot is taken, the two players rebound until player 2 scores or player 1 gains possession of the ball. When player 1 does, he passes quickly to the coach in the outlet area and tries to get free for a return pass from the coach. Player 2 tries to deny the return pass to player 1.
4. After player 1 receives the ball back from the coach, he or she tries to drive up court to the midcourt line (or for a score) against the defense being played by player 2.
5. Player 1 goes to line 2, player 2 goes to line 1, and the next two players in the lines continue the drill.

Teaching Points

1. Defensive players must move to get ahead of the dribbler without fouling (no reaching).

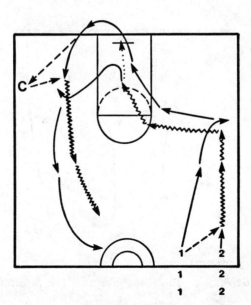

FIGURE 9-5   Recovery to the Defensive Position against a Dribbler

2. Player 2 must make a strong denial defense after the pass is made to the coach.

Drill 6   Three Men—Three-on-Two Situation

1. Three defensive players are positioned near the free-throw line with their backs to the coach, who has the ball at the baseline.
2. Three offensive players are positioned facing the coach.
3. Coach rolls or throws the ball to one offensive player. In this diagram, player 3 moves to pick up the ball. The defending player behind player 3 sprints to the baseline and then races down court. After gaining possession of the ball, player 3 dribbles as quickly as possible to the far basket for a layup or passes ahead to teammates 1 and 2, who have moved into the side lanes.
4. Offense goes into a three-on-two situation.

Teaching Points

1. Team defense communication.
2. Three-on-two situation until the defensive trailer gets back.
3. Picking up open man.
4. Playing three-on-three coming back the other way.

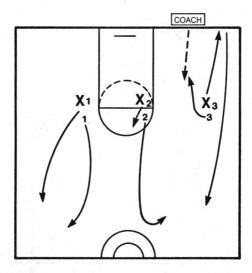

FIGURE 9–6   Three Men–Three-on-Two Situation

Drills 7 and 7A Three-on-Two Offensive Attack
Changes to Two-on-Three Attack vs. Pressure Defense.

1. Players 1, 2, and 3 attack from halfcourt and try to score against players X1 and X2.
2. Player 1 passes to player 3, who either shoots a jump shot or, as in this diagram, drives for a layup.
3. As soon as the ball starts to drop through the net, offensive players 1, 2, and 3 move quickly to their positions in a pressing defense.
4. Player X2 gains possession of the ball, steps quickly out-of-bounds, and passes to player X1, who has moved to the outlet area.
5. Players X1 and X2 may make any moves they desire to try to advance the ball at least two steps across the midcourt line.
6. Players 1, 2, and 3 try to double-team the ball and move to cover either player X1 or X2 in the passing lane. The double-teaming continues until

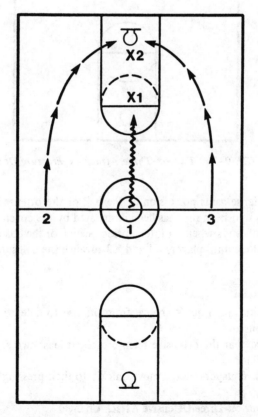

FIGURE 9–7a Three-on-Two Offensive Attack

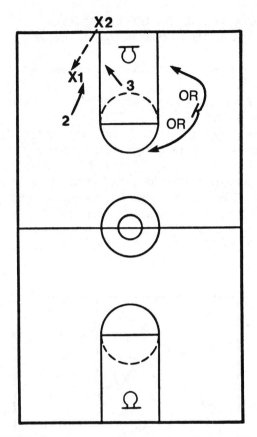

FIGURE 9–7b   Two-on-Three Attack vs. Pressure Defense

the defense gains possession of the ball or the offense has advanced the ball to a position that has been designated by the coach.
7. The drill ends when an interception occurs, or the coach may direct that it continue until players X1 and X2 advance the ball successfully.

Teaching Points

1. Stress making a quick change from offense to defense and from defense to offense.
2. Be sure that the offensive team crosses at least two steps over the mid-court line.
3. Defensive players should move quickly to their pressing positions.

**Drill 8   Four-on-Three Offensive Attack Changes
to Three-on-Four Attack vs. Pressure Defense**

1. Players 4 and X3 are added to Drill 7.

2. Player 4 is the offensive trailer and is positioned at the hash mark. Player 4 starts the cut toward the offensive end of the court as soon as player 1 starts the dribble toward the foul circle.
3. Player X3 is the third defensive player who must sprint to the defensive end of the court as soon as player 1 starts the dribble. Player X3 is positioned at the hash mark across the court from player 4.
4. After a score, players X1, X2, and X3 attempt to advance the ball up court against the four defenders (players 1, 2, 3, and 4).

Teaching Points

1. Quick change from offense to defense and from defense to offense.
2. The need to know exactly where to set up in defensive and offensive positions.
3. Quick recovery by the extra defensive man.
4. Alert movement to an open area by the offensive trailer.

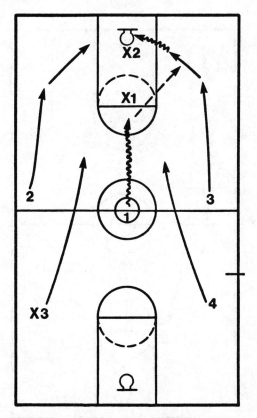

FIGURE 9–8 *Four-on-Three Offensive Attack Changes to Three-on-Four Attack vs. Pressure Defense*

5. These drills may be conducted over the full court as well as on the halfcourt.

Note: The two preceding drills may also be constructed so that there may be a five-on-four situation or a six-on-five situation. The coach's imagination will be the determining factor in how he arranges his players.

Drill 9   Stopping and Avoiding the Double Team

1. The team is divided into three lines as indicated. (Line X2 may also be placed near the midcourt circle.)
2. Player 1 dribbles quickly toward midcourt but is forced to stop as player X1 moves into his path. As player 1 stops the dribble, player X2 races to form a double-team situation with player X1 against player 1.
3. Player 1 attempts to avoid the double-team pressure by: a) pivoting away and passing to the post man or to line 1, b) passing quickly to an open teammate just before the double team occurs, or c) splitting the two defenders at the seam of the double team and making a quick pass to the post man.

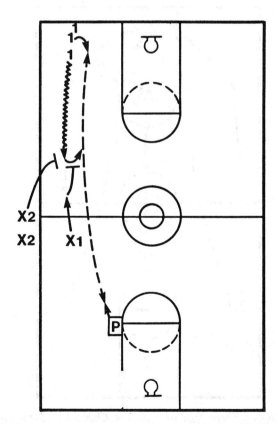

FIGURE 9-9   Stopping and Avoiding the Double Team

4. Player 1 goes to line X2, player X2 goes to line X1, and player X1 goes to line 1.

Teaching Points

1. The person with the ball should keep it under control.
2. Players should pass before the double team has occurred.
3. The ball handler should keep his head and eyes up.
4. Correct hand and foot positions and spacing by the double-teamers should be used.

Drill 10   Five-Man Recovery–Intercept and Pass Ahead

1. Five players are positioned in the foul lane, facing the basket. The coach is positioned at the foul-line extended area and has possession of the ball.
2. On the signal "go" from the coach, the five players sprint to the defen-

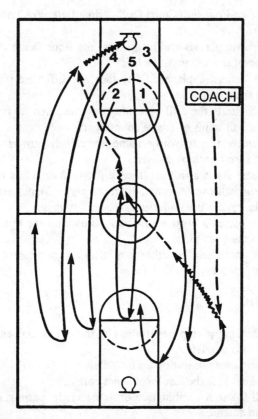

FIGURE 9-10   Five-Man Recovery–Intercept and Pass Ahead

sive end of the court. As the players reach midcourt, they turn and shuffle backwards so that they will be able to see the ball.

3. The coach will throw or roll the ball in the direction of one of the players (in this diagram, player 3 recovers the ball). As player 3 gains possession of the ball, he calls "ball," which signals his teammates to change direction and break up court as offensive players ready to receive a pass.

4. Player 3 should pass ahead to the first open man he or she sees. In this diagram he passes to player 5, who passes ahead to player 4, who makes the layup shot.

5. As soon as the ball goes through the basket, the players start playing defense. The coach may direct the team to retreat to a halfcourt zone defense, use full court zone press, and so on. The players must move quickly to their positions in the team defense.

Teaching Points

1. Making an immediate change from offense to defense.
2. Passing ahead to the open man.

Drill 11   Five-on-Four Full Court Drill—Add a Defensive Trailer

1. Five offensive players are lined across the floor facing the coach, who is at the top of the key with the ball.

2. The five defensive players (X's) face the offensive players with their backs to the coach.

3. The coach starts the drill by calling out one defensive player's name and passes the ball to his offensive counterpart.

4. The defensive player, whose name was called, must race to the endline and then sprint back on defense.

5. The offense starts a fast break with player 2 dribbling to the middle or passing the ball to a teammate (here, to player 3); players 1 and 4 fill the outside lanes; 2 is the trailer and 5 the safety man.

6. Defensive player 2 must sprint back to pick up the opponent or make a switch to the open man.

7. The drill continues the other way after a shot attempt (a score by the offense or recovery by the defense).

Teaching Points

1. The defense must stop penetration by the offense and enable player 2 to get back into the defense.
2. Stress team communication by the defense.
3. Players should fill the fast break lanes correctly.
4. This drill is also a combination drill: it includes passing, dribbling, filling lanes, and defense.

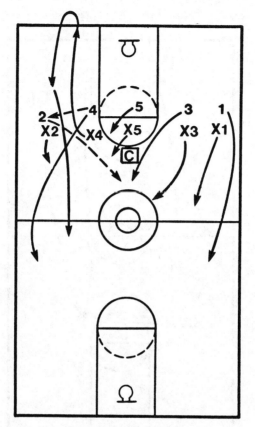

FIGURE 9–11   *Five-on-Four Full Court Drill–Add a Defensive Trailer*

Drill 12   Recovery to Defense

1. Two lines of players are positioned on the baseline at the end of the free-throw lane. The first two players in each line move into the free-throw lane and wait for the coach's signal to begin the drill.
2. Two coaches are positioned as indicated—at the wing positions near the sideline at each end of the court. Coach 1 has a ball in his possession, and he will be responsible for giving the signal to start the drill.
3. When coach 1 signals "go," the first two players sprint toward the basket at the opposite end of the court. After crossing midcourt, the players turn and look to see where the ball is. As the players make their turn, coach 1 throws or rolls the ball in their direction, and they react to gain possession of the ball. Player 3 picks up the ball and passes quickly to coach 2.
4. After player 3 passes the ball to coach 2, both players sprint toward the basket at the other end of the court, turn after crossing midcourt, and

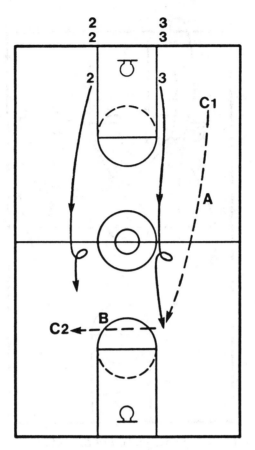

FIGURE 9-12   Recovery to Defense

look for the ball as they retreat toward the basket. Coach 2 throws the ball toward the players, who react to pick up the ball and pass it to coach 1. They then sprint to the opposite end of the court to continue the drill for a specified number of times before moving to the end of the lines.

5. The next two players in the lines step into the lane and run the drill.

Teaching Points

1. The players must react quickly when changing from offense to defense and must sprint toward the basket they are defending. They must think first of defending the basket area and then be ready to react toward the ball (or to the player with the ball).
2. Emphasize that the players should pass quickly to the coaches and react immediately by moving to the defensive end of the court.

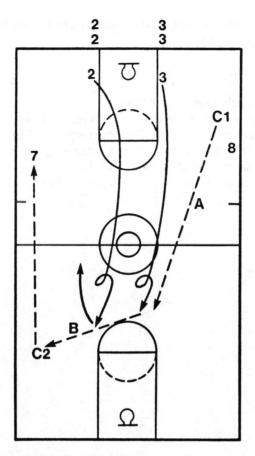

FIGURE 9-13 Recovery to Defense

Drill 12A Recovery to Defense

1. The players are positioned as in Drill 12; two additional players, 7 and 8, are added to the drill and positioned at the sideline near the time-line hash marks.
2. On the signal by coach 1, who has the ball in his possession, players 2 and 3 sprint toward the defensive end of the court. The players turn and look to see where the ball is located and react to recover the ball when it is thrown in their direction.
3. The player who recovers the ball passes quickly to coach 2, and both players sprint to the opposite foul lane, ready to defend the basket and to move out to defend against players 7 and 8.
4. Coach 2 passes to either player 7 or 8, who will try to score against players 2 and 3. Players 2 and 3 move out to defend against players 7 and 8 and prevent the score.

5. The players continue to play until a score is made or until the defense recovers the ball.

Teaching Points

1. Stress quick recovery to defense.
2. Emphasize that the defensive players must recover to the foul-lane area, since the basket is their first responsibility. They must approach the player with the ball quickly and aggressively but also cautiously, so as not to allow penetration to the basket.
3. The weak-side defensive player must move to a helping position.

10

Fast-Break Drills

INTRODUCTION

When the team is proficient in using the fast-break offense, it is the easiest and fastest way to score. To most people, the score resulting from a fast break is very exciting and a product of spontaneous and unorganized movement. But on the contrary, this type of system is not installed overnight. The fast break should contain specific patterns and rules that can only be developed through training.

A good fast break must include strong defensive rebounding, good passing, and well-conditioned players. The ideal fast break consists of a succession of fast, accurate passes, with dribbles used only when absolutely necessary.

The coach should explain and demonstrate to the players that a team offense may best take advantage of their opponents by pushing, or forcing the ball up the floor very quickly, before the defense has had a chance to get into position. The coach must also explain that well-drilled teams learn to recognize when a fast-break opportunity no longer exists and will move into a set pattern.

This chapter deals with the development of a fast-break system, which begins with rebounding and outlet-pass drills, progresses to halfcourt drills that include filling the lanes and scoring, and is completed with full-court continuous action drills.

REBOUND RECOVERY

Drill 1 Driving Layup

1. Players are positioned in a single line at midcourt, and each player has a ball (if possible).
2. The coach is positioned at the top of the free-throw circle.
3. Player 1 dribbles very quickly toward the basket and uses a crossover dribble to move past the coach and go in for the layup. Player 1 gets the rebound and dribbles quickly back to the line at midcourt.

Teaching Points

1. Players should protect the ball when making the crossover dribble.
2. The dribbler should use head-and-shoulder and eye fakes while approaching the coach.
3. Players should make a quick first step past the coach after the crossover has been made.
4. Players should make a strong accurate layup.

Drill 2 Drive, Stop, and Jump Shoot

1. Players are positioned as in Drill 1.

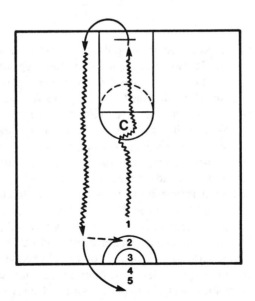

FIGURE 10-1 Driving Layup

2. Player 1 dribbles hard to the foul line, stops under control, and shoots a jump shot.
3. Player 1 rebounds his own shot and returns to the line at midcourt.
4. The coach is in a position that allows him to remind the jump shooter to use correct form when stopping and shooting.

Teaching Points

1. Dribbling very quickly and making an on-balance stop before shooting the jump shot.
2. Reacting quickly to recover the rebound before the ball touches the floor.

Drill 3 Jump Shot from the Wing or Corner Position

1. Players are positioned as in Drill 1.
2. The players dribble left or right and shoot a jump shot over the coach and manager, who are positioned about six feet from the side of the lane and foul-lane block.
3. Each player recovers his or her own rebound and returns to the shooting line.

Teaching Point

1. The shooter must stop and square his position to the basket (turn and face the basket) so that he is on-balance when taking the shot.

OUTLET PASS

Drill 4 Jump Shot and the Outlet Pass

1. Players are positioned as indicated in the diagram.
2. Player 1 dribbles hard toward the wing position and player X1 moves out to stop his penetration.
3. Player 1 shoots the jump shot and prepares to react toward the rebound. Player X1 blocks out player 1 and then moves quickly to the outlet area on the opposite side of the foul lane.
4. Player X2 rebounds the missed shot or recovers the made shot and makes a quick outlet pass to player X1.
5. Player X1 pivots and passes to the next player in line 1, who continues the drill.
6. Player X2 stays in the rebounding position for a designated number of shots. Player 1 goes to line X1, and player X1 goes to line 1.

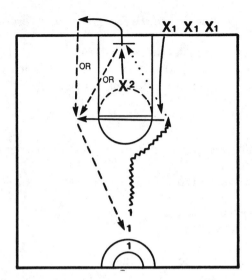

FIGURE 10-2   Jump Shot and the Outlet Pass

Teaching Points

1. Proper balance and form when stopping and going up with the jump shot.
2. Quick reactions by player X2 to recover the rebound and make the outlet pass.
3. Quick reactions by the defender of the outlet area.

**Drill 5   Jump Shot, Outlet Pass, and
Rebounder to Bother Outlet Pass**

1. The players are positioned as in Drill 4 with the addition of an offensive rebounder, player 2.
2. Player 1 dribbles to the position to the right of the foul line, where he is met by player X1, and shoots over the defensive man, player X1. After shooting, player 1 moves across the lane to the outlet area in order to receive the pass from player X2.
3. Player X1 is only responsible for bothering the shooter and does not rebound.
4. Player X2 recovers the rebound after blocking out player 2. Player 2 will also bother player X2's attempted outlet pass from either in-bounds or out-of-bounds.
5. Players 2 and X2 stay in the rebounding positions for a designated number of shots.
6. Player X1 goes to line 1, player 1 goes to line X1, while players 2 and X2 change positions.

Teaching Points

1. Using correct form on the jump shot.
2. Making a quick outlet pass.
3. Moving to the outlet area for the pass.
4. Using proper blocking out technique.

SCORING DRILLS

Drill 6   One-on-One with Trailer

1. One line of players is positioned at midcourt. The players will work in pairs on offense.
2. One defensive player is positioned at the foul line.
3. Player 1 dribbles toward defensive player X1. Player 2 follows player 1 slightly behind to the right and close enough for a handoff.
4. As player 1 reaches the defensive player X1, player 1 should hear player 2 calling out "trailer right."
5. Player 1 should then dribble to the left to get player X1 to move with him and drop a pass to player 2 for a layup. Player 1 may also dribble to the right, depending upon how to defensive player reacts to the movement.
6. If player X1 plays the trailer, player 2, player 1 drives to the hoop.
7. The drill should end with two-on-one rebounding, and either a score made by the offense or possession gained by the defense.

Teaching Points

1. Stress communication between players.
2. Stress drawing defense to the ball.
3. Emphasize rebounding by all players.

Drill 7   Fast Break, Dribble, Stop, Shoot over the Defense

1. Players are positioned in three lines as indicated.
2. Player 2 passes to player 1, who will drive hard toward the foul lane. After passing to player 1, player 2 moves to a position near the foul line so that he may prevent player 1's drive and force him or her to take a jump shot.
3. Player 3 rebounds and makes the outlet pass to the next player in line 2. If the shot is made, player 3 retrieves the ball as it comes through the basket and steps out-of-bounds to make the pass to the next player in line 2.
4. Player 1 goes to line 3, player 2 goes to line 1, and player 3 goes to line 2.

FIGURE 10-3 Fast Break, Dribble, Stop, Shoot over the Defense

Teaching Point

1. Use correct stop after dribbling and go up for the shot from a balanced position.

Drill 8 Fast Break, Reverse-Dribble,
Stop, Shoot over the Defense

1. Three lines are positioned as indicated in the diagram.
2. Player 2 passes to player 1, who drives toward the foul line after receiving the pass.
3. After passing to player 1, player 2 moves to stop the dribbler.
4. Player 1 drives, using a crossover dribble, when player 2 cuts off the path to the basket. After making the crossover dribble, player 1 starts to penetrate again, but player 3 steps into his path and forces him to take a jump shot.
5. Player 1 goes to line 3, player 2 goes to line 1, and player 3 goes to line 2.

Teaching Points

1. Using a correct crossover dribble, protecting the ball from the defense.
2. Protecting the ball and getting quickly into shooting position after coming to a stop.
3. Going up straight for the jump shot.

FIGURE 10-4   Fast Break, Reverse-Dribble, Stop, Shoot over the Defense

**Drill 9   Jump Shot from the Side Position–Shoot
for the Rim or Shoot for the Backboard**

1. Two lines of players are positioned at midcourt; each player has a ball in his possession.
2. Each player drives very hard to the forward position (about twelve to fifteen feet), stops on-balance, and shoots a jump shot.
3. The players recover their own rebound and move to the line on the opposite side of the court.

Teaching Points

1. Stress stopping on-balance.
2. Players should shoot the shot off the backboard, directly over the rim.

**Drill 10   Middle-Man Reaction Drill–Shoot,
Drive, or Pass on a Verbal Signal**

1. The players are positioned in two lines as indicated.
2. Player 1 passes to the coach and cuts quickly to the foul-line area. Player 2 cuts toward the wing position as player 1 makes his cut.
3. The coach makes a return pass to player 1. Just as player 1 receives the pass, the coach calls out either "drive," "shoot," or "pass." Player 1 reacts to the coach's signal.
4. Both players 1 and 2 rebound the shot and shoot until the ball goes in. They return the ball to the midcourt line.
5. Player 1 goes to line 2, and player 2 goes to line 1.

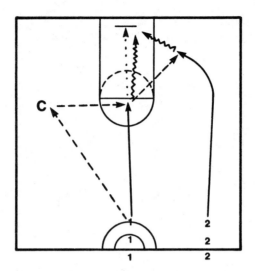

FIGURE 10-5   *Middle-Man Reaction Drill—Shoot, Drive, or Pass on a Verbal Signal*

Teaching Points

1. Stress making a quick reaction to the coach's signal.
2. Techniques of all types of passes should be emphasized.
3. Stress shooting techniques and the quick release.

**Drill 11   Layup—Drive to the Basket
and Look Back to the Middle**

1. The players are positioned in two lines, as in Drill 9.
2. Player 1 drives strongly toward the basket. As he approaches the foul-line area, player 1 picks up the dribble, makes a head-and-eye fake (looks) toward the middle, and then goes up for the layup.
3. Player 2 starts his drive only after player 1 has taken the shot, so that collisions are avoided.

Teaching Point

1. Players should use a good eye fake in order to freeze the defender or to make him react toward a possible crosscourt pass.

**Drill 12   Drive to the Basket from
Various Angles—One Dribble Drive**

1. Players are positioned in two lines. Player 1 is in possession of the ball and starts to drive toward the foul line.

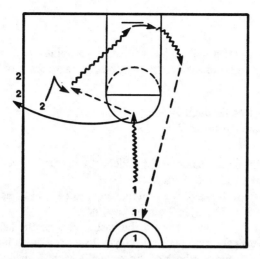

FIGURE 10-6 *Drive to the Basket from Various Angles—One Dribble Drive*

2. As player 1 dribbles toward the foul line, player 2 fakes toward the basket and then steps to receive the pass from player 1 after player 1 stops. Player 2 receives the ball, turns, and drives hard for a layup shot.
3. Player 2 recovers his own shot, passes to line 1, and goes to the end of line 1. Player 1 moves to the end of line 2.

Teaching Points

1. Player 2 must move as player 1 dribbles and then step to the ball just as player 1 stops the dribble.
2. Player 2 should drive low and hard to the basket and try to reach the basket after only one dribble.
3. This drill may be done from a variety of angles.

**Drill 13 Drive to the Basket—Defensive
Player Added to Cause Offensive
Player to Pull Up for Jump Shot**

1. Players are positioned as in Drill 12, but a third man, player 3, is added as defense.
2. Player 2 receives the pass from player 1 and starts to drive to the basket. Player 3 steps into his path to the basket just as player 2 starts his drive.
3. As player 3 moves to stop player 2's penetration, player 2 stops, gains his or her balance, and shoots a jump shot over player 3's attempt to bother the shot. Player 3 rebounds and passes out to line 1.
4. Player 1 goes to line 2, player 2 goes to line 3, and player 3 goes to line 1.

Teaching Point

1. Player 2 must regain balance after stopping his dribble and jump up straight to avoid the defensive man as he takes the shot.

Drill 14   Clear Through by Wing
Man for Baseline Jump Shot

1. Two lines are positioned at midcourt with each player in line 1 in possession of a ball. (See Drill 10.)
2. Player 1 dribbles to the foul-line area, stops, fakes a pass to the right, and then passes to player 2 on the baseline.
3. Player 2 cuts hard toward the basket, crosses the lane, and prepares to receive a pass from player 1. Player 2 shoots a quick jump shot.
4. Players 1 and 2 rebound, shoot until a score is made, bring the ball out to midcourt, and change lines.
5. The next players begin as soon as a score is made.

Teaching Points

1. The player who cuts through to the baseline must be ready to receive the pass and prepared to shoot a quick jump shot.
2. The shooter learns whether to shoot off the board or directly at the rim.
3. The shooter should be moving to receive the ball by the shooter.
4. All players should rebound aggressively.

Drill 15   Clear Through by Wing
Men for Baseline Jump Shot

1. Three lines are positioned at midcourt.
2. As player 1 dribbles to the foul line, players 2 and 3 cut toward the basket and cross over to positions on the baseline.
3. Player 1 may pass to either player 2 or 3 after faking to the opposite wing.
4. All players rebound and continue shooting until a score is made.
5. Player 1 goes to line 2, player 2 goes to line 3, and player 3 goes to line 1.

Teaching Points

1. Stress passing techniques.
2. The receiver should be ready for the pass and ready to shoot quickly.

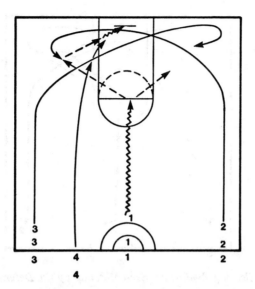

FIGURE 10-7 Clear Through by Wing Men for Baseline Jump Shot

Drill 16 Clear Through by Wing Men and Pass to the Trailer

1. Add player 4 to Drill 15. Player 4 delays the cut toward the basket; he or she counts "one-thousand-one, one-thousand-two" and then cuts down the side of the lane, ready for a pass from player 2.
2. All four players rebound.
3. The players rotate to different lines, or the coach may use only the big men on the team in the trailer position.

Teaching Point

1. The trailer must time the cut down the lane so that he or she will receive a pass in position to make an effective shot.

Drill 17 Scoring Against an Even Matchup by the Defense—Pass and Screen on the Ball

1. Players are positioned in three lines at midcourt simulating the second phase of the fast break.
2. Player 1 passes to player 3 and moves to set a screen for him.
3. Player 3 receives the pass from player 1, fakes a baseline drive, and then drives toward the middle. Player 3 uses the screen by player 1 to free himself from defensive player X.

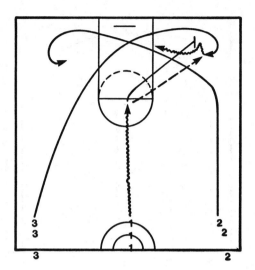

FIGURE 10-8 *Scoring Against an Even Matchup by the Defense—Pass and Screen on the Ball*

Teaching Points

1. Stress correct screening position.
2. The player with the ball should make a proper fake and drive off the screen.

Drill 18   Scoring Against an Even Matchup by the Defense—Pass and Go Behind for a Handoff

1. Players are positioned as in Drill 17. Player 1 passes to player 3 and moves quickly to a position behind him or her for a handoff return pass.
2. After making the return pass to player 1, player 3 cuts toward the basket. Player 3 may set up in the pivot position or may move across the lane, either to set a screen or to clear the right side of the court for player 1.
3. Player 1 may shoot over a screen by player 3, may drive to the basket, or may pass inside to player 3 or to a player cutting from the weak side of the court.

Teaching Points

1. Proper handoff.
2. Correct cut to receive the handoff.

Drill 19 Scoring Against an Even Matchup
by the Defense—Dribble-Screen and Handoff

1. Players are positioned as in Drill 17. Player 1 drives toward player 3, ready to set a screen against defensive player X and then pass or hand off to player 3.
2. Player 3 fakes toward the baseline and then cuts behind the screen set by player 1. He receives the handoff pass from player 1 and drives to the basket. (Player 3 may also shoot a jump shot or pass to player 1, who has rolled toward the basket after screening.)

Teaching Point

1. Stress correct screen and handoff.

Drill 20 Scoring Against an Even Matchup
by the Defense—Pass and Screen Away

1. Defensive players X2 and X3 are added to the formation for Drill 15 and are positioned near the foul-lane blocks. These positions may be filled by the coach, manager, or players.
2. Player 1 passes to the right to player 3 and then cuts away from the ball to set a screen on defensive player X2.
3. Player 2 makes a fake toward the baseline and cuts toward the ball, ready to receive a pass from player 3.

Teaching Points

1. Stress correct screening position by player 1.
2. Player 2 should make a proper fake and cut off the screen.

FILL THE LANES, HALFCOURT

Drill 21 Filling Lanes

1. Players 1, 2, and 3 are in a single line in the free-throw lane with player 1 in possession of the ball.
2. On a signal by the coach, player 1 starts to dribble toward midcourt, while players 2 and 3 fill the lanes.
3. The emphasis here is to fill the lanes properly by cutting wide and staying close to the sidelines. The drill ends at midcourt and the players return to starting positions.

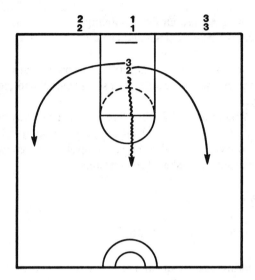

FIGURE 10-9 Filling the Lanes

Drill 22 Gaining Possession of the Defensive Rebound and Making the Outlet Pass

1. The players are positioned in two lines as indicated. Also, one player (6) is positioned near the sideline at the foul-line extended area.
2. Player 1 throws the ball against the backboard and jumps to gain possession of the rebound. Player 1 gains control of the rebound, returns to the floor, pivots, and passes quickly to player 6 in the outlet area.
3. Player 6 passes the ball to player 2, who will be the next rebounder, and then moves to the end of the rebounding line. Player 1 replaces player 6 as the outlet pass receiver.

Teaching Points

1. The rebounder should go up strongly for the ball.
2. Do not allow the rebounder to bring the ball below chest height. The coach is positioned so that he may observe and correct this technique.
3. The outlet pass may be one of a variety of passes used.
4. The receiver should be in the correct outlet position.

Drill 23 Clear the Rebound to the Corner

1. The players are positioned in two lines at the sides of the free-throw lane. Also, there is a player stationed at the free-throw-line extended area on each side of the court.

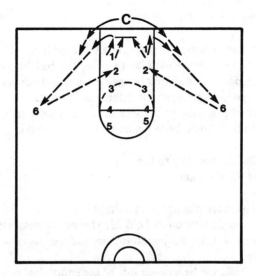

FIGURE 10-10 *Gaining Possession of the Defensive Rebound and Making the Outlet Pass*

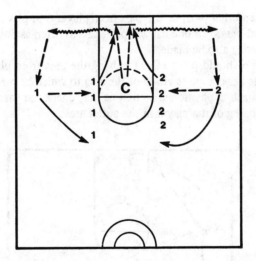

FIGURE 10-11 *Clear the Rebound to the Corner*

2. The first player in each line, 1 and 2, throws the ball against the backboard and jumps to gain possession of the rebound. The player then looks to the outside of the court.
3. Players 1 and 2 fake an outlet pass, then proceed to dribble out to the corner.
4. The players come to a stop, pivot, and pass to the player in the outlet area.

Teaching Points

1. The rebounder should go up strongly for the ball.
2. Do not allow the rebounder to bring the ball below chest height. The coach is positioned so that he may observe and correct this technique.
3. Stress making a good, strong dribble to the corner.
4. The outlet pass may be one of a variety of passes used.
5. The receiver should be in the correct outlet position.

Drill 24   Outlet Pass, Pass to the Middle, and Fill the Lane

1. The players are positioned in a single line.
2. This is a continuation of Drill 23. The second pass is made from player 6 to player 5, who moves toward the midcourt area with a quick control dribble.
3. Player 6 fills the lane on his side of the court after passing to player 5.

Teaching Points

1. The centering pass, or the pass from player 6 to player 5, must be a two-handed pass or a one-handed push pass as often as possible so that a fake move may also be made.
2. Player 6 should pivot after receiving the pass from player 1 and be sure that he has complete vision of the area to which he plans to pass.
3. The coach is positioned so that he may check the passing techniques and positioning of the player in the outlet area.

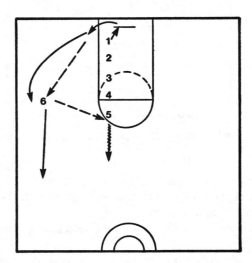

FIGURE 10-12   Outlet Pass, Pass to the Middle, and Fill the Lane

Drill 25 Outlet Pass, Fake the Centering Pass, and Dribble to the Middle

1. The players are positioned in a single line as in Drill 24.
2. Player 6 fakes a pass to player 5, who cuts toward the center court and then to the sideline if he does not receive the pass.
3. Player 6 drives strongly toward the midcourt area to fill the center lane, while player 5 moves into the right lane.

Teaching Points

1. The pass receiver should pivot, fake a pass, and drive quickly toward the middle. Using a long first step he or she pushes the dribble out in front so as to move quickly past any defensive player in the area.
2. The coach should be sure to remind the dribbler to keep the head up so that the whole court can be seen and also to avoid the defensive player when he or she starts the dribble.

Drill 26 Outlet Pass After the Escape Dribble Toward the Corner

1. The players are in a single line as in Drill 24. An additional person, X, is added to the drill. X may be the coach, manager, or player.
2. Player 1, the rebounder, is prevented from making a direct outlet pass by defensive player X. Player 1 takes one or two quick dribbles toward the corner in order to clear himself away from the defensive player.
3. Player 1 passes to player 6 and replaces him in the outlet area. Player 6 moves to the end of the rebounding line after returning the ball to the next player in line.

Teaching Points

1. The rebounder should give maximum protection to the ball as he makes a hard, low dribble toward the corner.
2. The pass from the rebounder should be quick—a one-hand push pass or a baseball pass.

Drill 27 Blastout Dribble Against Defensive Pressure

1. The players are positioned near the basket and in the lane. Player 1 has possession of the ball and tosses the ball against the backboard.
2. Player 1 rebounds and looks to make an outlet pass to either player 3 or 2, both of whom are near the sidelines. Players X4 and X5 prevent the outlet pass.

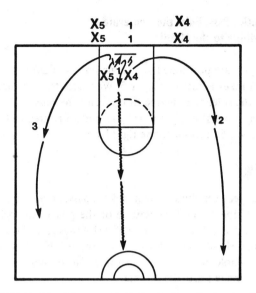

FIGURE 10-13   Blastout Dribble Against Defensive Pressure

3. Player 1 then splits the two defensive players by using a strong dribble toward the midcourt area. As player 1 dribbles between them, players X4 and X5 break to fill the outside lanes for a full court or halfcourt break.

4. Player X5 goes to line 1, player 1 goes to line X4, and player X4 goes to line X5. Players 2 and 3 remain in these positions for three or four plays and then change places with two players in lines 1, X4, or X5.

Teaching Points

1. The dribbler should push the ball in front of him and try to reach the foul line with one dribble.

2. Players X4 and X5 must sprint to fill the lanes and be ready to receive the pass from the dribbler.

Drill 28   Outlet Pass After the Blastout Dribble

1. Players are positioned as in Drill 27, with players 2 and 3 breaking to the outlet areas from positions near the foul line.

2. Player 1 escapes the double team by players X4 and X5 and passes ahead to either player 2 or 3, both of whom are breaking to the outside lane positions as they see player 1 start his drive away from the defense.

3. Player 1 sprints to fill the middle lane after passing ahead to player 2, or cuts behind player 2 to fill the right lane if player 2 dribbles into the middle.

4. Players X4 and X5 make their moves to fill the lanes or to become the trailer and safety man.

Teaching Points

1. Players 2 and 3 do not break to the outlet areas until player 1 gains possession of the rebound.
2. The rebounder must pass ahead as quickly as possible to the open man.

Drill 29 Outlet Pass to Sideline Outlet Area or Center Outlet Area

1. Players 1 and 2 are positioned at the defensive guard positions, and player 5 is the defensive rebounder.
2. Player 5 tosses the ball against the backboard and jumps strongly for the rebound.
3. As player 5 gains possession of the ball on the left side of the basket, player 1 breaks to the outlet area on the sideline and player 2 breaks toward the middle of the foul lane.
4. Player 5 passes to either player 1 or 2, depending upon the pressure being applied by player X.

Teaching Points

1. The rebounder must react to the pressure by the defense and pivot away from the pressure in order to clear himself to make a pass.

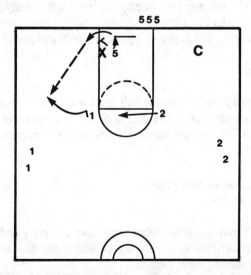

FIGURE 10-14 Outlet Pass to Sideline Outlet Area or Center Outlet Area

2. Players 1 and 2 do not break to the outlet areas until player 5 has control of the rebound.

Drill 30   Outlet Pass After the
Clearout Dribble to the Corner

1. Players are positioned as in Drill 29, but with two defensive players bothering the rebounder.
2. Player 5 uses an escape dribble toward the corner in order to clear himself for the pass to player 1.

Teaching Point

1. The coach may use only the bigger players or key rebounders in the player 5 and player X positions and alternate them. Also, the coach may use only guards or outlet men in the player 1 and player 2 positions.

Drill 31   Fill Lanes After In-Bounds Pass—After
a Score from the Three-Man Weave

1. The players are positioned in three lines at midcourt. Player 1 passes to player 3, who passes to player 2, who in turn returns the pass to player 1. Player 1 shoots a layup shot.
2. The shooter, player 1, recovers his or her own made shot, steps quickly out-of-bounds and makes a pass to either player 2 or 3, who have both moved to the outlet areas. After making the pass, player 1 cuts opposite from the direction of his pass.
3. In this drill, the pass goes to player 3, who will quickly return the ball to the middle man at midcourt.
4. Player 1 goes to line 3, player 3 goes to line 2, and player 2 goes to line 1.

Teaching Points

1. The shooter must recover the ball quickly and get it back into play.
2. The player who makes the pass in-bounds can go away from the ball or to the ball side, in accordance with the coach's direction at the beginning of the drill.

Drill 32   Fill Lanes—Four Players—
After the Outlet Pass

1. Players 3 and 4 are the rebounders, and players 1 and 2 are the outlet men. All four players are positioned within the lane and are alert to recover a long or a short rebound.
2. In this drill, the manager shoots and player 4 rebounds the ball.

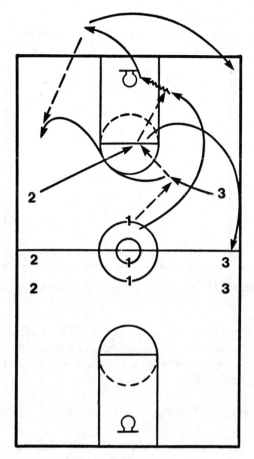

FIGURE 10-15 *Fill Lanes After In-Bounds Pass—After a Score from the Three-Man Weave*

3. As soon as player 4 gains possession of the rebound, player 2 moves to the sideline outlet area and player 1 moves to the foul-line area and then toward the midcourt area.
4. Player 3 sprints to fill the third lane.
5. Player 4 passes to player 2 and player 2 passes to player 1. Players 2 and 3 fill the lanes and player 4 becomes the trailer.
6. Players rotate lines at the completion of the two passes.

Teaching Points

1. The players do not move to outlet areas until possession of the ball is gained.
2. Players should keep lanes filled and stay wide.

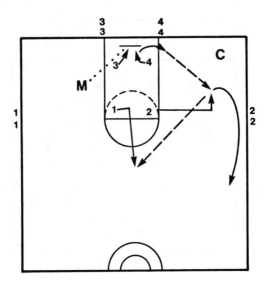

FIGURE 10-16   Fill Lanes—Four Players—After the Outlet Pass

3. The outlet man should move to the ball to receive the pass after break-ing to the sideline. This player should try to keep his back to the sideline as he receives the pass; this will give him maximum vision so that he may see the whole court.

Drill 33   Fill Lanes—Five Players

1. Players are positioned as in Drill 32, with a fifth player added. Here the manager shoots from the opposite side of the court and player 3 rebounds.
2. All players break to an area of responsibility and fill the lanes.

Teaching Point

1. This and the previous drill may be conducted with an insert or rebound ring on the basket so as to guarantee a rebound.

Drill 34   Clear Through by Wings and
Pass to the Trailer by the Dribbler

1. The players are positioned in three lines as in Drill 15.
2. A fourth player is added and is positioned between the middle man and the wing man. This player (4) will delay the cut, as he or she will be the trailer.
3. Player 1 fills the center lane using the dribble, while his teammates, players 2 and 3, cross through the lane because they are very much ahead of the ball.

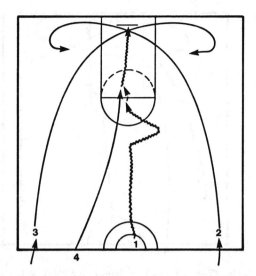

FIGURE 10-17 *Clear Through by Wings and Pass to the Trailer by the Dribbler*

4. Player 1 dribbles to the right corner of the foul lane for the purpose of clearing a cutting lane for the trailer, player 4. Player 4 receives a soft pass from player 1 and drives for the layup.

Teaching Points

1. The correct timing of the trailer's cut should be emphasized.
2. Player 1 should make a soft, accurate pass.
3. A verbal signal, such as "left" or "right," may be used by the trailer to indicate to player 1 on what side the cut is being made.

**Drill 35 Clear Through by Wings
and Weak-Side Cut by the Trailer**

1. The players are positioned as in Drill 34.
2. Player 1 drives and passes to player 3, who has crossed through the lane to the right side.
3. Player 4, the trailer, moves down the left side of the lane and then cuts across the lane toward the ball. Player 3 passes the ball to player 4 for a layup or a hook shot.
4. Players rotate lines after the shot.

Teaching Points

1. The timing of the trailer's cut toward the ball and into an open area should be stressed.

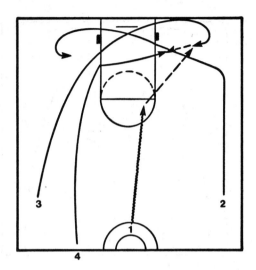

FIGURE 10–18   *Clear Through by Wings and Weak-Side Cut by the Trailer*

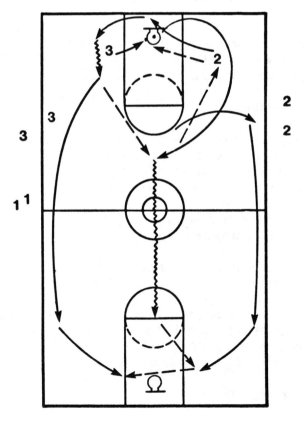

FIGURE 10–19a   *Filling the Lanes*

2. Player 3 should make a quick, accurate pass.
3. Stress keeping the lanes filled and staying wide.

FILL THE LANES, FULL COURT

Drill 36 Filling the Lanes

1. The players are positioned in three lines as indicated.
2. Player 1 passes to player 2, who in turn passes to player 3. Player 3 shoots a layup shot and then cuts toward the top of the key.
3. Player 2 recovers the ball after player 3's layup shot, takes two quick dribbles to the side, and passes to player 3 at the top of the key.
4. After passing to player 2, player 1 moves to the outlet area on the right and then moves up court to fill the left lane.
5. The three players move up court to shoot at the far basket and continue the drill at that basket.

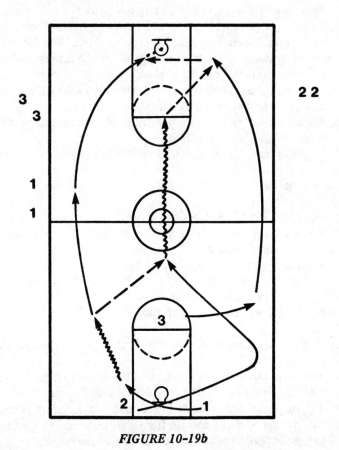

FIGURE 10-19b

6. Player 3 passes to player 1, who passes to player 2 for the layup shot. Player 1 recovers the pass, dribbles toward the sideline, and passes to player 2, who has cut to the top of the key.
7. Player 3 moves to the outlet area and then fills the right lane.
8. The drill may continue as many times as the coach designates.

Teaching Points

1. Emphasize quick passing.
2. Players must sprint to fill the lanes.

Drill 37   Fill Lanes from Single Line—Return with Outlet Pass After the Score—Pass Ahead

1. Players 1, 2, and 3 are in a single line, at the baseline, with player 1 in possession of the ball.
2. Player 1 dribbles down the court, and players 2 and 3 fill the lanes.
3. Player 1 passes to player 3, who shoots a layup and recovers his own shot.
4. Player 3 steps out-of-bounds and passes to player 1, who moves to the outlet area. Player 2 crosses under the basket and fills the left lane on the return up court. After passing, player 3 fills the lane on the right side.
5. After receiving the pass from player 3, player 1 drives toward midcourt and then passes ahead to player 2, who drives for a layup shot or passes crosscourt to player 3, who will shoot the layup.
6. Player 1 must race to gain possession of the rebound or made shot before the ball touches the floor.
7. Player 1 goes to line 3, player 3 goes to line 2, and player 2 goes to line 1.

Teaching Points

1. Players should fill the lanes quickly.
2. Stress making a correct pass to the cutter going for the layup.
3. Stress making the layup.
4. Emphasize making a proper outlet pass.

Drill 38   Outlet Pass, Get the Ball to the Middle, Fill Lanes, Take the Layup Shot

1. This is a full court continuation of Drill 37. The players are positioned in three lanes.
2. The player who rebounds gives a quick outlet pass to the wing man; or a dribble to the corner, then passes to the outlet area.
3. The wing man pivots, looks to the middle of the court, and gives a quick pass to the forward coming from the weak side to the middle. After giving the pass, he continues to run wide up the court.

4. The rebounder fills the opposite side lane.
5. The player in the middle dribbles to the opposite free-throw line and gives a pass to either of the wing men for a layup shot.

Teaching Points

1. Good quick accurate passes should be emphasized.
2. Players should keep the lanes wide.

Drill 39   Fill Lanes from a Jump-Ball Situation

1. Player 5 moves into the circle and is the jumper in a jump-ball situation.
2. Players 2 and 3 are positioned at the sides of the circle, ready to receive a tip from player 5 and start the fast break.
3. The coach tosses the ball, and player 5 tips the ball to player 2. Player 2 goes for the ball, gains possession and starts the break by driving toward midcourt.
4. Players 3 and 5 move to fill the lanes.

Teaching Point

1. Players 2 and 3 must react to the ball and gain possession before starting the fast break.

SHOOTING DRILLS

Drill 40   Fast-Break Layup Drill

1. Players are positioned in two lines as indicated. The coach has a ball and is assisted by a manager, who will receive the ball from the players and relay them to the coach.
2. The coach rolls the ball in any direction; the first player in line 1 races to scoop the ball and drive for the layup shot. Player 1 retrieves the rebound, dribbles quickly to the sideline, and uses a speed dribble to return to line 2, where he passes the ball to the manager.
3. As soon as player 1 shoots the layup, the coach rolls the ball for the first player in line 2. Player 2 scoops, drives, shoots, and then retrieves the ball and returns to line 1.

Teaching Points

1. Players should be sure of possession when they scoop the ball.
2. Stress making a hard, quick drive for the layup.

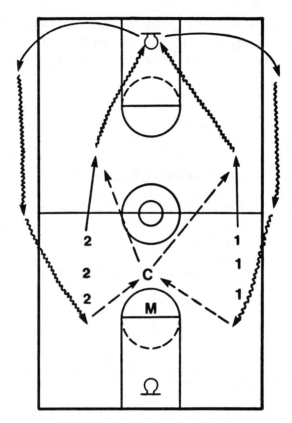

FIGURE 10-20   Fast-Break Layup

Drill 41   Fast-Break Layup and Outlet Pass

1. The players are positioned in two lines as in Drill 40, and then a third and fourth line are added at the fast-break outlet areas.
2. The coach rolls the ball to player 1, who scoops and drives. After player 1 recovers the rebound, he makes a quick outlet pass to player 3. Player 3 uses a speed dribble back to the end of line 2 and returns the ball to the manager. Player 1 goes to the end of line 3.
3. The drill continues with player 2 scooping and driving for the layup and making an outlet pass to player 4.

Teaching Point

1. Quick reaction to recover the rebound or made shot—the shooter may step quickly out-of-bounds to make the pass after recovering a made shot.

Drill 42 Layup Shot, Outlet Pass, and Return the Pass to the Trailer

1. The players are positioned in two lines at midcourt. Each player in line 1 has a ball.
2. Player 1 dribbles strongly for a layup shot and then breaks to the outlet area near the foul-line extended area.
3. Player 2 follows the shooter, gains possession of the rebound or made shot, steps out-of-bounds, and passes to player 1 at the outlet area or makes an outlet pass after rebounding. Player 1 dribbles quickly up court to the foul line and comes to a stop. After passing to player 1, player 2 runs quickly up court and receives a pass from player 1 as he makes his cut from the right wing position.
4. Player 2 either drives for a layup or shoots a jump shot.
5. Both players rebound, return to the lines at midcourt, and exchange positions.

Teaching Points

1. Players should fill the lanes quickly.
2. Players should get the ball into play very quickly after the made shot.
3. Players should get under control and on-balance when taking the layup or jump shot.

Drill 43 Fast Break, Layup Shot, Outlet Pass, Bother the Rebounder, and Chase the Break

1. Players are positioned in two lines at midcourt, as in Drill 42, but player 3 is added.
2. Player 1 passes to player 2, who is on the move toward the basket. Player 2 receives the pass and drives hard for a layup.
3. Player 1 follows player 2 to the basket and recovers the rebound or made shot. If player 2 makes the layup, player 1 steps quickly out-of-bounds to make an outlet pass to player 2, who has moved to the outlet area. Player 3 bothers the pass by player 1. If the layup is missed, player 1 rebounds the shot and makes a quick pass to player 2 in the outlet area. Player 3 also bothers the rebounder's outlet pass attempt.
4. After player 2 receives the outlet pass, he speed-dribbles to the foul line at the opposite end of the court. Player 1 fills the lane behind player 2. Player 3 chases the play and attempts to bother the pass and/or shot being made by players 2 and 1.
5. All players rebound: player 2 goes to 3, player 1 goes to 2, and player 3 goes to 1.

Teaching Points

1. Emphasize making a correct outlet pass with pressure on the passer.
2. The rebounder should react quickly to make the outlet pass and fill the lane.
3. Player 3 must be aggressive when bothering the passer and then must recover quickly to the defensive end of the court.

Drill 44   Fast-Break Jump Shot

1. The players are positioned in four lines as indicated.
2. Player 1 starts the drill by driving hard toward the basket. Player 4 moves out to stop player 1's drive and tries to force him to take a jump shot. Player 1 shoots and player 4 rebounds the shot.

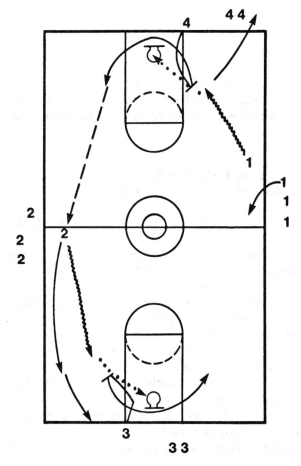

FIGURE 10-21   Fast-Break Jump Shot

3. Player 4 passes out with a long baseball pass to player 2, who is near mid-court. Player 2 drives hard for a layup but is forced to stop and take a jump shot as player 3 moves out to stop the penetration. Player 3 rebounds the shot and passes, using a baseball pass, to player 1.
4. Player 1 goes to line 4, player 4 goes to line 2, player 2 goes to line 3, and player 3 goes to line 1.

Teaching Points

1. The shooter should be in control and on-balance and go up straight for the jump shot.
2. Stress making good passes.
3. Footwork on defense should be emphasized.
4. Stress making a good outlet pass.

Drill 45 Fast-Break Jump Shot—Run, Stop, Shoot

1. Players are positioned in three lines as indicated.

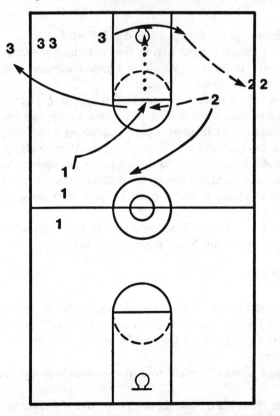

FIGURE 10-22 Fast-Break Jump Shot—Run, Stop, Shoot

2. Player 1 cuts quickly toward the foul-line area and receives a chest pass from player 2. Player 1 shoots a quick jump shot.
3. Player 3 rebounds the shot and makes a quick outlet pass to line 2. The next player in line 1 cuts toward the foul line just as player 3 makes his pass to player 2.
4. Player 2 goes to line 1, player 1 goes to line 3, and player 3 goes to line 2.

Teaching Points

1. Player 1 cuts to the foul line with the hands ready to receive a pass and provide player 2 with a target.
2. Player 2 must pass to player 1 in a position that will allow player 1 to make a quick shot.

TEAM DRILLS

Drill 46   Pass Out–Pass Ahead–Step
to Meet the Pass

1. Five lines of players are positioned as indicated.
2. Player 1 throws the ball against the backboard, rebounds, and makes an outlet pass to player 2. As player 1 gains possession of the ball, player 2 fakes and steps to meet the pass.
3. As the pass is made from player 1 to player 2, player 3 makes a fake toward midcourt and then steps to meet a pass from player 3. Player 4 fakes and comes to meet a pass from player 3, and player 5 fakes and comes to meet the pass from player 4. After receiving the pass from player 4, player 5 drives hard for a layup, recovers the ball, steps out-of-bounds, and speed-dribbles up the sideline to take his or her place in line 1.
4. The next player in line 1 starts his play after player 5 drives for the layup.
5. Player 1 goes to line 2, player 2 goes to line 3, player 3 goes to line 4, player 4 goes to line 5, and player 5 goes to line 1.

Teaching Points

1. The receiver steps to meet the pass and gives the passer a target by extending his hand and arm. He or she should catch the ball on the move and then pivot toward the middle of the court so that he can see the receiver.
2. The pass should be made to a receiver who is on the move toward the passer.
3. Players should move quickly to an open area after passing.
4. Correct use of the speed dribble should be emphasized.
5. Players should concentrate on making the layup.

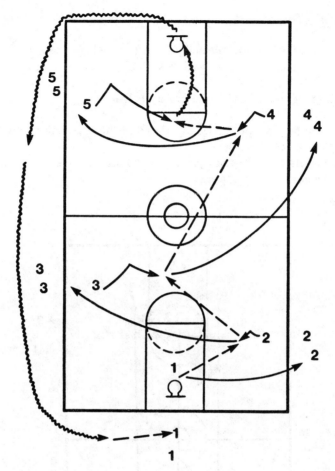

***FIGURE 10-23** Pass Out—Pass Ahead—Step to Meet the Pass*

Drill 47   Baseball Pass and Speed Layup

1. Two lines are positioned at midcourt near opposite sidelines, line 1 facing toward the basket and line 2 facing the opposite basket.
2. One player is positioned under each basket, and each player has a ball.
3. These two players start the drill by dribbling quickly to the foul circle and stopping to throw a baseball pass to the first player in each line, who is cutting to the basket. A player does not start his cut until the dribbler-passer reaches the foul line.
4. The player who receives the pass drives for a layup, recovers the ball, dribbles to the top of the key, stops, and throws a pass to the next player, who cuts to the basket.
5. Players go to the end of the line to which they pass.

Teaching Points

1. The dribbler must stop and gain his balance before passing.
2. Players should throw a lead pass.

Drill 48   Two-on-One Full Court Passing Drill

1. Two lines are positioned at the end of the court and a third line (X3) is located at the sideline.
2. Players 1 and 2 attack player X3 and attempt to score at the other end by using a series of passes.

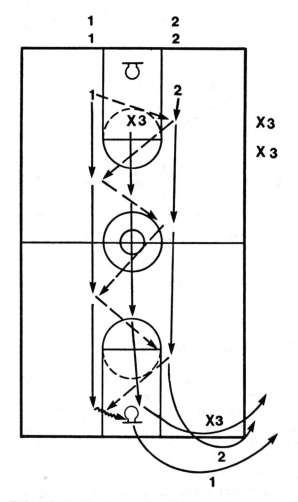

FIGURE 10-24   Two-on-One Full Court Passing Drill

3. As players 1 and 2 get closer to the offensive basket, they try to force player X3 to commit himself so that one of the offensive players may get free for an easy layup shot. The layup shot is what the offense must make in a two-on-one situation.
4. The players rebound until the score is made and then move to the sidelines. Player 1 goes to line 2, player 2 goes to line X3, and player X3 goes to line 1.

Teaching Points

1. Stress quick passing.
2. Players should draw the defensive player toward them as they approach the top of the key with the ball.
3. Stress making the layup.
4. The defensive player must bluff and force the offense to stop, hesitate, or take a jump shot—not a layup.

Drill 49   Fill Lanes—Five-Man Break—Positioning the Trailer and Safety (Defensive) Player

1. The fundamentals exercised in the previous drills should be stressed again.
2. The two new aspects that are added in this drill are the player in the trailer position and the player in the safety position.
3. In the drill, players 1, 2, and 4 fill the lanes, with the ball in the middle lane.
4. The player who rebounds will usually be in the safety position or will stay back at midcourt for defensive purposes.
5. The last rebounder becomes the trailer, following the ball down the middle lane. The trailer moves as close as possible to the player in the middle when he stops at the free-throw line.
6. As the trailer approaches the player with the ball, the trailer yells "right" or "left," depending on which side. The trailer receives the pass for a layup.
7. The drill continues to the other end of the court.

Teaching Points

1. Quick, accurate passes should be emphasized.
2. Players are to fill the lanes and stay wide to keep the court open so that it is more difficult for the defensive players.
3. There should be communication between the trailer and the player with the ball.
4. There should always be a player back in the safety position.

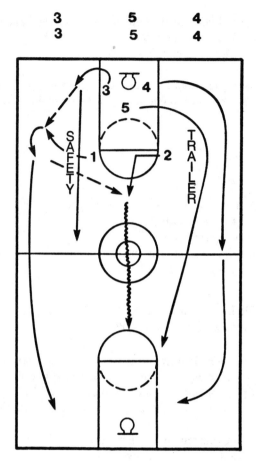

FIGURE 10-25 *Fill Lanes—Five-Man Break—Positioning the Trailer and Safety (Defensive) Player*

Drill 50   Continuous Action Fast Break Drill

1. Players are positioned as indicated with the numbers playing together in one group and the X's playing together in another group.
2. Player 1 passes to player 2 and receives a return pass from him as the drill begins. As the first pass is made, defensive players X1 and X2 run to their defensive positions in the key and try to stop the fast break.
3. When the offensive team moves the ball past the time-line hash marks, player 4 moves into the drill as an offensive trailer. Player X3 also moves onto the court at this time and becomes a third defensive player.
4. The break continues until the defensive team recovers the rebound on a missed shot or takes possession after the offensive team has scored a basket. (See note at the end of this drill.)

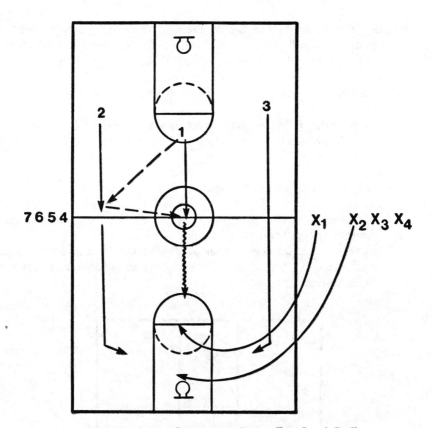

FIGURE 10-26 *Continuous Action Fast-Break Drill*

5. Player X2 rebounds a missed shot and makes a short, quick pass to teammate X1, who is breaking to the outlet area. Offensive players 2 and 3 bother the rebounder so that the pass will be made under game conditions.

6. Offensive players 1 and 4 retreat to the defensive end of the court, ready to defend against the break.

7. Player X3 breaks toward the outlet area and then to the middle of the court for a pass from player X1. Player X2 fills the opposite lane after making the outlet pass to player X1.

8. The drill continues as a three-on-two situation until the offensive team and the ball have passed the time-line hash marks.

9. At this point, player X4 becomes the offensive trailer and player 5 becomes the third defensive player. Players 2 and 3 go to the end of their team's line.

10. The drill continues until the defense gains possession and starts the fast break in the opposite direction.

Note: After a score by the offense, the same two players who bothered the rebounder (in this diagram players 2 and 3 bothering player X2) will attempt to pressure player X2, who has taken the ball out-of-bounds after the score.

Teaching Point

1. Each phase of the fast-break game appears in this drill, and the coach may choose to emphasize certain parts or all phases of it on a particular practice day.

Drill 51   Three-on-Two Continuous Action

1. The team is divided into groups of three players as indicated. These groups stay together during the drill.
2. Players 1, 2, and 3 start a break against players X1 and X2 whose teammate, player X3, is positioned in the outlet area and does not get involved in the defense.

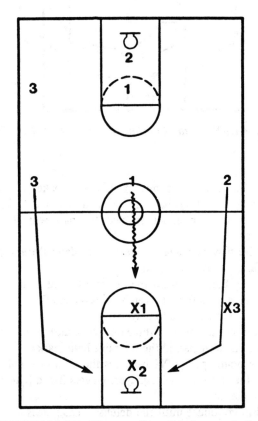

FIGURE 10-27   Three-on-Two Continuous Action

3. Players X1, X2, and X3 make a fast break the other way after gaining possession of the ball. They break against players 1 and 2 and their team-mate, player 3, who is in the outlet area.
4. Players 1, 2, and 3 move into the defensive positions after players X1, X2, and X3 break.
5. The three players alternate their positions during the length of the drill, which will be determined by the coach.

Teaching Points

1. Stress the various fast-break responsibilities.
2. Players should keep lanes wide and filled.
3. Stress defensive work and try to prevent layups and second shots.

**Drill 52   Three-on-Two—Break
and Recover from Five Lines**

1. Five players are positioned in the lane close to the basket. The players face toward the basket as if in a blockout position. The players are given a number from 1 to 5.
2. The coach, who has possession of the ball, calls two numbers and then throws the ball to one of the other players (player 3 receives the ball in this diagram).
3. When players 2 and 5 hear their number called, they react immediately and sprint to the other end of the floor to defend against the three-man break by players 1, 3, and 4.
4. At the completion of the break, the five players line up in the lane and break back up court after the assistant coach has called the numbers and made the first pass.
5. The coach may devise other variations of the drill which will determine how the players return to their starting positions.

Teaching Points

1. Stress a quick reaction to defense.
2. Stress a quick reaction by the offense to fill the lanes and move the ball up court.

**Drill 53   Eleven-Man Continuous Action Fast-Break
(Endurance) Drill—Rim Insert May Be Used**

1. Players 1, 2, and 3 break against defensive players 4 and 5. All five players rebound. The player who gains control of the rebound makes an outlet pass to either player 6 or 7. The rebounder breaks with players 6 and 7 up court against players 10 and 11.

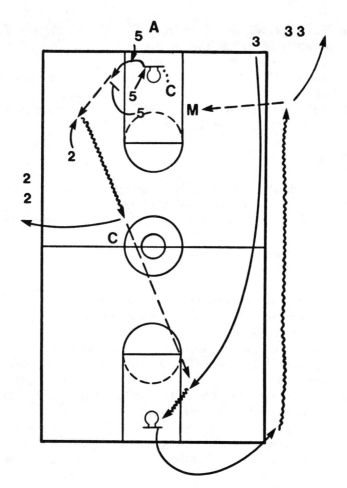

FIGURE 10-28   Outlet Pass with Long Lead Pass

2. All five players—10, 11, 6, 7, and the rebounder—go for the rebound. The player who gains control of the rebound makes an outlet pass to either player 8 or 9 and breaks with them up court against players 1, 2, 3, and 4, who fill the two defensive positions and the outlet areas.

Teaching Points

1. Emphasize aggressive rebounding.
2. Players should fill the lanes correctly and make a proper outlet pass.

Drill 54   Outlet Pass with Long Lead Pass

1. Players are positioned in three lines as indicated. Line 5 rebounds, line 2 receives the outlet pass, and line 3 is the shooting line.

2. The coach or manager tosses the ball against the backboard. A second person (manager) stands at the side of the lane with a second ball, in a position to receive the ball being returned by player 3.
3. Player 5 rebounds the ball, using correct technique, and makes an outlet pass to player 2. The type of outlet pass may vary—a two-handed overhead, baseball, or push pass after an escape dribble. One player from line 5 (5A) is positioned on the baseline ready to try to steal or deflect the ball if player 5 brings the rebound down below chest height. Player 5B attempts to bother the outlet pass. After a specified number of turns, the players in line 5 exchange positions.
4. Player 2 steps in-bounds and is ready to move to meet the pass from player 5 as he sees him gain possession of the rebound. Player 2 then pivots and starts to drive up court. After two quick dribbles, he stops on-balance and makes a lead pass to player 3 for the layup. He must be aware of the defensive player (C) or a teammate.
5. Player 3 starts on the baseline in the deep corner opposite the rebounder. As player 5 gains possession of the ball, player 3 sprints to the other end of the court on a line to the basket, ready to receive the pass from player 2 and drive for a layup shot. Player 3 rebounds the player 3 shot and dribbles back to the line, using a speed dribble.

Index

DATE DUE

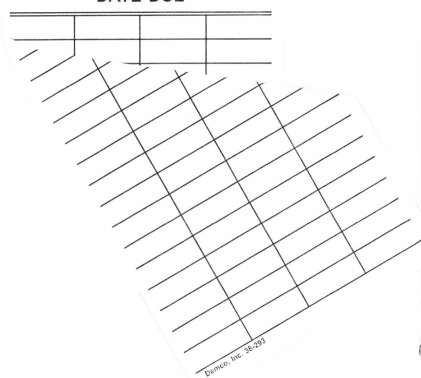

Demco, Inc. 38-293